MW00324575

Powerful voice of the Great Plains...

"To be sure, he is a humorist. His puckish wit, his satire and audacity have long had his readers laughing out loud. But Tony's ability to mesmerize readers with essays which touch on the losses in life, is equally remarkable. As readers have laughed over the years with Bender, so have they shed tears.

Tony's stories, his original style, are a distinct reflection of life on the prairie. Call him a humorist, a philosopher if you will. He is both. Tony Bender is a powerful new voice from the Great Plains."—*Allan Burke, publisher, Emmons County Record, Linton, ND*

Tony Bender is a treasure...

"Tony Bender is a treasure. Humor writing, I've been told, is the most difficult form. You wouldn't believe that when reading Tony's stories. They seem so effortless and so dead on. And when he writes one of his poignant pieces, he captures not only the soul of the subject, but also of the reader. Dave Barry would like him for his humor and Charles Kuralt would've admired him for his empathy. He's an artist who uses words and paper. And you'll be able to admire his art when you read this book."
—*Jim Hornbeck, publisher, Daily News, Wahpeton, ND*

Brilliant...

"Brilliant and engaging."—*Nancy Berry, Golden Valley News, Beach, ND*

A great story teller...

"The columns were touching and hilarious as the author marched inexorably through his memories. A great story teller."—Colorado Newspaper Association, *judges of the 1992 N.D. Better Newspaper Contest, awarding Bender's one of seven first place awards his column won in the 1990s.*

Laugh or reflect in silence...

"Tony's view of the world and the people in it is often unique. He has the wonderful ability to translate those views into stories that can make you laugh out loud or reflect in quiet silence. Tony's story telling talent has been a welcome addition to our newspaper for many years. His columns are a constant source of compliments from our readers."—*Lynn Schroeder, publisher, Cavalier Chronicle, Cavalier, ND*

One of those rare writers...

"Whatever the profession, the truly talented people make what they do look effortless. Likewise, Tony makes great writing look effortless. He's one of those rare writers capable of deeply touching the full spectrum of human emotions.... nothing makes us feel more alive then when we experience the full range of emotions."—*Patrick Kellar, publisher, Connersville News-Examiner, Connersville, IN*

Loons in the Kitchen

Humorous and Poignant Short Stories From the Dakotas

by Tony Bender

Cover photography and design by Tony Bender
Edited by Jane Haas

Loons in the Kitchen

International Standard Book Number: 0-9705442-0-0

Published by:

Redhead Publishing
PO Box 178
Ashley, ND 58413

1-701-288-3531

redhead@drtel.net
www.ashleynd.com
www.wisheknd.com
www.tonybender.com

Printed in the United States of America

Foreward

I would write. That was always the plan I laid out early in my life. First I would embark on a radio career, travel, seek adventure, and then, when I had grown too old to be cool on the radio, I would settle down and write.

That was the plan. Of course, as a youth, I also planned to sin like a son of a gun until the day I died, when in all sincerity I would repent and go to heaven.

Some plans must be abandoned along the way.

When I began writing newspaper columns in 1990, it was all part of the plan to polish my skills for the novel I planned to write. In the beginning, people wondered if I wanted to be "another Wayne Lubenow," a veritable legend of a writer whose column appeared in many small weekly newspapers in North Dakota. At first I rejected the comparison despite my fondness for his writing.

After his death in 1991, in a column entitled, *I'm Not Wayne*, I wrote about the changing of the guard: *Well, Wayne, your work is finished and ready or not, it's time to make way for the brash Young Turks. It's the way of the world, and you know, Wayne, I have to believe that you were once brash and invincible too.*

A lot has happened in 10 years. I am less brash. And decidedly mortal. As I sifted through hundreds of columns for this collection, I was able to measure where I have been as a writer and where I am now. I remain a work in progress as one elderly lady informed me one day.

"I read your column every week," she told me, her nose a mere inch from mine.

I beamed.

"Sometimes it doesn't make any sense!" she asserted.

There have been experiments that failed.

I never wanted to be categorized strictly as a humor writer or as a writer of more serious fare. My readers never knew what to expect. Their loyalty allowed me the freedom to write what I feel. There is laughter and there is pathos on these pages. Some pieces are irreverent. Others are intensely personal—so personal that sometimes I hesitated to publish the piece. But I always did.

Dusting off the memories contained in this book has been a stirring task. Resurrected here are stories of uncommon men and women of the Dakotas. I have always loved these prairies, and I have embraced the individualism, the stoicism and the wry humor of those I have met in my travels.

Publication of this book represents the close of a chapter and the beginning of a new one. While I intend to continue my weekly epistles, I will also begin my first novel, which has been brewing and fermenting in my brain for all these years. The characters in the unwritten book have been patient while I wrote these stories.

This book and its memories are where I have been.

Now it is time to move on.

—*Tony Bender*

Dedication

For Julie (a.k.a. The Redhead) who provides balance, humor and inspiration to my life.

For Dylan, who has made me a better person.

For India, another jewel in my life.

And for Gunnar. We miss you so much.

Thanks

To Dad, for the genetic stubbornness that allowed me the confidence to challenge the norm—even you. And thanks for your quiet pride when I proved you wrong.

To Mom, for always keeping my feet on the ground and reminding me when I boasted of home runs and RBIs, that "The pitcher wasn't very good, was he?"

To Bernice Rollo, my high school English teacher, who first hinted that if I was not yet something special, I could be.

To Connie Groop, former editor of the *Brown County News*, for giving me space and a start.

To Wayne Lubenow for opening my eyes to the possibilities. I regret we never met.

Contents

Lives Collide

Dawn. Golden-orange sunlight streamed from the east, slamming into rugged buttes rising out of the prairie.

Strange to see so much beauty, to feel so much peace as my old Bronco lumbered to the scene of terrible misfortune. Duck, my Brittany Spaniel, had his nose buried in the can of pet food and didn't seem to notice.

I arrived at the ranch an hour early, and a woman came to the door. I introduced myself, we discussed the weather and she invited me in.

The house was small and homey. Breakfast was on the table and Lucille invited me to share. Coffee would be fine.

I waited until they were through before I asked any questions about the crash. Until then, we shared personal information—the kinds of things only residents of the plains can talk about within minutes of meeting. Wilmer and Lucille had three grandchildren. I was going to be a father for the first time. Years separated us. Tragedy had brought us together.

Outside, just half a mile away in a stubble field, the crumpled plane lay, and I almost forgot about it as Wilmer talked of the new calf he'd brought into the world. He spoke slowly, a rich dignified voice, his eyes betraying the strain of many calving seasons. It had been a hard week. The road washed out yesterday. But he got it filled in. Then the pipe to the water tank burst, and it had taken until 10 p.m. last night to get the damage repaired. Muddied hip boots dried in the porch.

And then there had been the awful discovery of the man and the plane. He must have been about Wilmer's age. For three weeks the wreckage lay so close but undiscovered.

Wilmer told me what he knew about the crash as I scribbled in the notebook. Just the facts... So antiseptic...

The son of the pilot would be here today, they said. My news story was someone else's family nightmare.

Wilmer spoke by radio with his son, 20 miles away, on another ranch. Two sleepy-eyed, bone-tired ranchers, discussing new calves and long hours. Interminable pauses separated the transmissions. Pauses that are only comfortable around family or close friends.

"I've got a reporter here," Wilmer said.

Pause.

A long pause.

Very long.

"Uh huh," said the son finally.

I hadn't noticed Lucille patiently waiting at the table. In her hands was a tattered black Bible. Three strips of silver duct tape held the cover together.

Wilmer waited patiently as I rattled on inanely about this and that. When I gave him a pause he said, "It's time for our morning devotional."

"You're welcome to join us," Lucille invited.

I would.

It was mighty fine praying. Lucille went first and she prayed for family. She prayed for friends. She prayed humbly and so sincerely. She prayed for me, "our friend, who has joined us." She asked for a blessing on my wife and for the one on the

2

way.

I was touched.

A little choked up.

A lot choked up.

A little teary eyed.

I croaked out a thank-you when she had finished. I had come seeking calamity and had been offered salvation.

When Wilmer began his prayer from his rocker, it startled me. "To get to the truth...may we live, honor and appreciate all you do for us." Here was a man dead-tired at dawn, a man who had faced a trying week, and he thanked God for it all. And he meant it.

"We think about the son that we will meet today," Lucille prayed. "Would you have your hand upon them today?"

God surely was listening.

I thanked them again, for sharing the moment. "We always invite people to stay. Some walk outside," she said. And then she smiled, a stray grey hair fell onto her forehead. "I'm glad you stayed."

At the crash site, the investigator was officious. From Chicago. But as we talked, he warmed up. He spoke of the sadness his job entails. But there was a lot of good in his life, too. There were the people he met. And the Prairie City cafe had good food.

He gazed at the miles of plains and buttes. He had been an artist. "It's so surreal. I know why you people live here," he said.

Then he seemed to remember Chicago.

"Don't ever leave," he ordered.

As I drove away, I thought about the grief-stricken son who would soon arrive. But I knew he'd be in good hands.

Like planes tumble from the sky, lives collide in the most unpredictable manner. An old man from Nebraska, a man we would never meet, had brought strangers together.

I drove by a church on the way home.

I drove by a school.

I had already been there.

© Tony Bender, 1996

Wednesday's Ashes

For the same reason people share laughter at funerals and cry at weddings, they gathered, and on the surface it seemed like a party as old friends shared memories about the church that now crumbled before them into an unholy brew of flame, smoke and cinders.

Soggy, yellow-jacketed firemen from four towns outnumbered the citizenry. That's the way it's been for a long time in Long Lake, SD it seems. The numbers are down to fifty or so now, and except on Friday nights when a bunch of Charlie Fischer's recruits gather for broasted chicken he calls in typical auctioneer bluster, "the very best you ever ate," crowds don't congregate here much anymore.

But today, as fire and time gnaw like relentless predators on their community, the witnesses gather, and the heat from the burning provides a final comfort against the raw wind.

The irony of the last church in town burning on Ash Wednesday is not lost on them. They smile at the cosmic joke—because you don't endure the way Long Lake has without a sense of humor.

In Long Lake, they whistle full sonatas in the graveyard. In Long Lake, even as the hangman tightens the noose, the condemned do Rodney Dangerfield "no respect" jokes.

"We take Ash Wednesday *serious* in Long Lake," Lucy Fischer deadpans.

"I was confirmed in that church," Charlie announces—as if he was the only one.

"I'm surprised it didn't burn *then*," comes the rejoinder, accompanied with a grin and a slap on his back.

Back in 1886, before hope was rationed in miserly portions, the first of five churches was established.

But over the years, clouds of grasshoppers and poverty drove many away from the parched land, and five churches became two. And in 1937, a tornado splintered Immanuel Lutheran Church. The church was rebuilt, but 30 years later that congregation joined this one.

To sanctify the union, like blood brothers, the two congregations built this church and in the steeple, they placed a bell from each parish.

The low-toned bell thumped your chest on Sundays. The high-toned bell joined in the song and called the angels to join the service. The sound was "beeeauoootifuuul," Charlie says, his German brogue betraying him, stretching the word out with three or four extra syllables.

There's not an Irish-Catholic for miles, but this most certainly is a wake. The memories flow like communion wine. Rudolph and Lucille Heyd's wedding was the first one held in the church back in 1938. There are no pictures of the event, he says. "Nobody had no money back then for pictures."

Lucille should be here for this. This is history.
But she's in the Wishek Nursing Home. "This was like our home," Rudolph sighs as he watches the front steps crumble.

When the last wall has fallen, old-timers point to the cornerstone where a tin box was tucked away 61 years ago. A fireman kneels on the ground, as if in prayer, and opens it. Inside, a leather-bound German Bible smolders. Gently he wets it down

6

and it is passed from hand to hand. Pastor Michael Jacobson holds it for a moment too.

It is his lot to comfort, to make sense of it all, and he tries. "The building is gone but the people are still here. The church has not disappeared from Long Lake," he says.

You want to believe.

You really want to believe.

© Tony Bender, 1999

Writer's note: The church was rebuilt after all. "It's beeeauooootifuuul," Charlie Fischer will tell you. But the bells were a total loss.

Dear Dylan

D ear Dylan,

I started composing this letter as I was driving you home from day care.

As usual, you greeted me with a smile when you heard my voice, but now you're sleeping, snug in your fuzzy yellow snowsuit as we bust through the pillow drifts on the gravel road that leads home.

It's hard to believe you're four months old already. And somehow, when your mom and I talked about being parents, we could never imagine you. You're really something.

You've taken over the house in a spectacular fashion; though, I think Duck Dog has been a little put out by all the attention you get. But in time, I'm sure that you'll be best pals tromping across the prairies, coming home with scraped knees, gopher tails and poison ivy.

It's still hard to think of myself as a dad, and it's even harder for me to think of your mother as a mom. She's such a career woman. Well, she's still a career woman, but you've changed her. And boy, are we both surprised. You've turned that long, cool redhead into a mushy, devoted mom.

And me. You've turned me into kind of a softy, too. I can't pretend to do half of your care, but I change lots of diapers, get up with you at 3 a.m. and I give you baths, too. I'm the one who tucks you in at night, and on Sundays, well, that's our day. You and me. We watch football just like I used to with my dad.

When you were born, someone asked my mom, your Grandma Jan, "What kind of father will he be?" She replied, "Anyone can be a father, but he'll be a daddy."

That meant a lot to me. Because I've rarely known her to be wrong about these things. But by the time you're able to read this, I'll have made lots of mistakes and you will have, too.

But we'll get through it.

Part of me can't wait to see you grow up, to see what you'll become. Another part of me is afraid that it's going to happen. I've known you for four short months, and I'm already dreading graduation.

You're going to live in a wonderful time. I really believe that. Though I don't think your mom and I really talked about it, having a baby, I think, is an expression of optimism. About our future and yours. It's hard not to be optimistic with you around, Dylan.

Well, Mom had to go to work early this morning, so it's just you and me. In a few minutes I'll be bundling you up for the trip back into town. Sometimes you doze on the way to day care. Other times you gaze over at me all the way into town, like I'm the most perfect guy in the world. I'll enjoy that feeling while I can. The time will come, as you mature, that you'll see my imperfections. That will mean you're growing up and thinking for yourself. That's the way the world works.

But in the end you'll still be my son and I'll still be your dad. And that can fix just about anything.

Love, Daddy

© Tony Bender, 1996

The Last Hunt

In the old days "Mac" McIntyre would issue the warning over KNDC airwaves: "Things are going to liven up in Hettinger this week. The boys from Ohio are coming!"

It was the official start of hunting season in Hettinger. To hell with official edicts from game and fish departments about the official opening—hunting season wasn't really official until Tommy Williams arrived from Toledo with his 12 gauge.

This was Tommy's secret paradise. A holy hunting ground whose secrets he was loathe to share. Asked back home where he managed to find all the good hunting, he'd tell 'em Fargo, Sioux Falls, Rapid City... anything but the truth.

And when hunting magazines started to leak the secret of Hettinger's abundant pheasant population, he was livid. Hadn't this dusty, dry little town been his discovery, hidden away between crew-cut buttes and rustling prairie grass?

For 44 years he'd come traipsing back to the plains for The Hunt. Now it was Mac's son, Al, who heralded the arrival of the "Ohio Boys" on the radio.

Mac was long gone like so many of the friendships Tommy had formed in annual pilgrimages in those seasons of brittle leaves.

So much had changed. So many faces gone. Sons had taken their place and Tim, Tommy's son, was here, too. Hard to believe Tim was 42. They'd been hunting here together since he was 11.

"It was so hard. All his great friends were gone," Tim says. Jake Wolf... Bill Clement... Mac... and "Doc" Fuglie.

Doc, oh man, what story...

Doc still lives in the old black and white movies Tommy's friend, Marty Belcik, shot of all the hunts. They shot birds. He shot movies.

The Ohio Boys had gone back to town that day and dragged Doc out of his office for some duck hunting. No time to change clothes 'cuz "They're flying good, Doc."

"Doc Fuglie's got his suit and tie on and he's shooting ducks," Tim laughs at the sublime absurdity of it all. "He's still got the tie on!" He roars as his eyes see again, in his mind, the silent flickering film where shotguns jolt shoulders but make no report.

Of course, now Marty's gone.

Only the images he captured remain.

Doc's gone, too.

But The Hunt. That was the constant. And this year, on opening day, Tommy was back. And Hettinger rose from the slumber that surely must overtake her when he wasn't here.

For all he knew, the town didn't live until he came back each fall to breathe life into the characters that performed just for him. For you see, a dream can't live without the dreamer.

"You couldn't live here," Tim explains. "That would ruin it." Indeed, the shine would wear off. But each year Tommy would rediscover his second home.

It was here that he bought 240 acres, just to be a part of the land. It was here that he would ask a farmer for permission to hunt—and then spend the next half hour talking about the grain. The cattle. The drought. He'd grown up on a farm, and Lord knows, he didn't want these folks thinking he was just another city slicker.

"He was outgoing. He was a conversationalist. He absolutely had that sincere interest in people," Tim explains. "He could be anywhere and strike up a conversation."

And when he returned to his job as maintenance supervisor at Sun Oil Refinery in Ohio, his heart—the one that suffered through three attacks in 1985—stayed behind.

Still, he came for The Hunt in '85. Tired. Not four months removed from the last heart attack, he was here. It was cold and the snow was deep—the going tough. "That was indicative of my father and his desire to hunt," Tim says. "He was dead. There's no way he should have lived. He was a tough bastard."

So it wasn't like they didn't expect something to happen. Orma, Tommy's wife, had his obituary ready for years. But each autumn, she let him go to his secret place. And each fall, she knew the phone might ring... "My mother was so unselfish to let him come out here," Tim says.

She loved him that much.

"This was his dream... If he was gonna go, he wanted to go here," Tim says. "We talked about it. We laughed about it—as much as you can laugh about death."

"The week before he died... The conversations we had... Now I understand. Because it was special."

He looks away, drinking in the vision, and he tells of driving with his father. Time had etched its mark on the athlete's body. "He looked kind of small," Tim says. Together they drove across the bleak, unforgiving Dakota tundra where biting winds had become a formidable challenge for the aged hunter.

"You know, Tim, I'm not sure about our forefathers..." Tommy said as he envisioned the covered wagons, sod houses and Indians that had once claimed the harshness his tired eyes now scanned. "I'm not sure if they were tough... or just stupid." The father and son laughed.

The final hunt was a good one. Tommy had dropped his limit of ducks the day before—two with one shot.

And on this opening day of ringneck season, he got his limit again. Again he had dropped two with one shot from the 20 gauge Browning he had gone to in concession to the years. "He just couldn't miss with that gun," Tim says. He hadn't missed in getting his limit. And his dog, Cutty, a 13-year-old Chesapeake Bay retriever, performed like a pup. She retrieved the last bird of the day. "He must have said it three or four times, 'This is the best I've felt in years,'" Tim recounts. "He'd had a great day, he really had."

And when Leo Miller's dog flushed the last pheasant of the day, Tommy admired the dog's work and walked up to shake Leo's hand. "That's a fine dog," he said. And then he collapsed. A stroke.

"That was typical of Father," Tim says, smiling, tears welling, "shaking a guy's hand, telling him what a good dog he had."

CPR started Tommy breathing again and in those frantic moments Cutty stood over him and barked. "Get up goddam it," Tim translates.

At the hospital, Dr. Mattson told Tim, "He might be able to hear you."

"I love you, Dad," Tim said to his father as he squeezed his hand. And in his darkness, Tommy heard. "He squeezed back... with his trigger finger," Tim says, choking back the tears.

It was his last signal to the world, but his heart beat on. "C'mon Dad, give it up," Tim implored as the days dragged on.

"Goddam Dad, give it up!"

But after Orma and Linda, Tim's sister, had arrived to say their goodbyes, the oxygen was turned off. And then, and only then, did that great heart stop beating.

Now Tim continues The Hunt but "I don't attack it with the same intensity. It's not that important for me to shoot anything."

For his elk hunt in Wyoming, ten days removed from the funeral, Tim loaded up his father's Remington 30-06, the one with open sights. Tommy didn't use a scope and this year neither will Tim.

Tim will be back for pheasant season in Hettinger next year. "Oh yeah. But I don't think I could do opening day... Too tough." He shakes his head slowly. "Too many memories..."

© Tony Bender, 1994

Writer's note: I had planned to write this story of Tom Williams a year earlier, but when the photos I took were botched in the darkroom, I decided to hold it a year.

After all, I knew Tommy would be back.

So I planned to write it the next year.

I saw Tim at a football game the next fall and told him I wanted to get together with his father and him in a day or so.

"There's plenty of time," Tim said just days before he lost his father. The words still haunt me. T.B.

All That Jazz

Feet aching, we settled into black metal chairs in the nondescript open air cafe just off Decatur Street.

Immense plastered columns supported the canopy that hid us from the sun. The iron was a delicious cool to my North Dakota skin.

Fat, battleship grey pigeons brazenly clucked and scrapped beneath our feet, fighting for crumbs.

Honey-sweet, the clarinet gave voice to the rhythm of the other three. The stand-up bass thumped, the drummer gently rapped, and on keyboards, a middle-aged woman with a crimson ribbon in her ebony-black hair, lightly delivered the chords.

Then, in her bright spring dress, she leaned ever-so-slightly into the microphone and started singing *Autumn Leaves.*

And I was gone. Splitsville.

We had come for the music and for the food. Salt shakers were idled, so exquisite were the spices and sauces on the catfish and oysters in the Big Easy.

And at every corner from Bourbon to Decatur, music skipped like a party hat through the pungent air. Bouncy zydeco. Heartbreak blues. And that jazz, all that jazz.

The Redhead had to nudge me as the flop-haired slouchingly handsome young waiter asked again for my order.

Voodoo. I would have N'awlins-brewed Dixie Blackened

Voodoo. The Redhead would have an ice tea.

My gaze returned to the band. The Redhead smiled at my obliviousness. I smiled back a far-away smile.

As I waited for my muddy-looking beer, I drank in the music, savoring each nuance, trying to hold the elusive notes, but they slipped away. My ears reached eagerly for each new fleeting note.

How can I describe the way she sang? A hint of Ella when she teased a high note for a beat. A touch of Sarah Vaughn's richness. The words do not exist to describe the moment.

With arrogance I have long thought of my craft as the perfect form of communication. The written word makes us more eloquent than we can ever hope to be in base conversation. We massage the sentences. We edit. We rethink. We rewrite. Paragraphs may take hours. And some days the residue on the pages is smarter, funnier, than we really are.

But words now fall inadequate—they stand by useless even as the moment remains vibrant in my mind.

I walked to the keyboards after the song. As I dropped a dollar in the tip jar, I leaned over to speak to the singer. She didn't hear me the first time, and she cocked her ear to me. I realized then she was blind.

She nodded and the clarinet player announced the song.

Waitresses joyfully bounced a hip-hop jig, ignoring customers with tapping feet. A couple danced, and I grinned as the man with the licorice stick added a melody that floated and darted between the lyrics of *Fly Me to the Moon* like young Muhammad Ali in the ring with a tomato can.

"...*Let me play among the stars.*
Let me see what spring is like on Jupiter and Mars.
In other words, hold my hand...

*In other words, Darling kiss me..."**

The clarinet sassed.

The singer scatted.

And I was gone.

In the next days, we heard the boisterous brass at Jackson Square. Shades of Louie.

We were lured into a Bourbon Street dive by a dancing bartender, the bebop piano and a pasty-faced sax player.

One drink minimum. Six-fifty for a beer. And it was a bargain. The well-rounded trumpet player stood front and center and when he played, people stopped on the streets to listen.

The Redhead bounced in her seat. And when the piano man played his eccentric chops, the trumpeter and the sax man looked over his shoulder in admiration.

And we were gone.

The last day our feet carried us back to that open-air cafe. This time we learned the singer's name—Jeannie Breazeale— and like the thirsty in a drought, we greedily drank in the tunes one more time.

A white-haired man stood listening, leaning over an upright piano. He leaned and listened so as not to miss even the subtle scratch of fingers on the bass strings. Divine it was.

As the clarinet player passed the hat, I asked them to play *I've Got the World on a String.*

He sighed the sigh of a man who has heard the question before, the sigh of a man who knows well the song would be so wonderfully caressed by the singer. "I've been trying to get Jeannie to learn that one," he said as he moved on.

When they were done playing, the singer stood, then shuffled a few steps to await the gentle guiding hand of the bass player.

He led her to a table in the sun, and she sat in prim, perfect posture with her back to us, a half-dozen abandoned wrought iron tables separating us.

Though it was time to return to the clattering century-old St. Charles streetcar for the last journey past the stately mansions of the Garden District, I lingered there in the shadows, watching the singer.

She could not see me smile.

© Tony Bender, 2000

* Music and lyric, Bart Howard

The Redhead's Tractor

It was The Redhead's idea that we get a tractor. Well, she didn't actually come out and *say* she wanted one, but a man gets to know his woman over the years. The next thing you know, she'll covet a Harley Soft Tail or a '67 'Vette.

This tractor business started two and a half years ago when we bought this home in the country. I feared this house. Like any 25-year-old house, it needed some work, but what really scared me was the yard. It rested on five acres of vegetation so thick I swear we were stalked by wild dingos as we walked the grounds.

"Well, at least it has a nice grove of trees," I allowed as we walked. "Actually, that's wormwood," it was explained.

We had a little talk, The Redhead and I, and she told me I loved the house and apparently, somewhere during the conversation, I convinced her we had to buy it.

That's when she told me she intended to turn the full five acres into a lawn. It was obvious then that she needed a tractor, but I, like all men, being a bit obtuse, didn't grasp her message at the time.

Soon after we moved in, we were courted by the neighbor who wondered if he could bale our yard like he had in the past. Now, it don't take a Rhodes Scholar to figure out that any yard that will provide enough hay to winter a herd of black angus isn't a yard really; it's more akin to a national grassland. In the interest of the cows, I suggested we maintain just a one-acre yard. Now, I don't know what those bovines ever did to The Redhead, but she turned me down flat.

So her parents donated their riding mower to the cause and bought a new one for themselves. And for the first two summers, a couple times a month, they would drive 90 miles with their mower on the trailer and help drive over wormwood trees.

Both mowers endured unspeakable tortures. Blades were mangled. Belts were shredded. Steering linkages unlinked. There was squealing and clunking so fierce, sometimes I was driven to rise from my computer to see what was happening.

I know this looks bad, but let me remind you that none of this was my idea. And I did pitch in. I always had dinner ready when they came in from mowing. And, in a moment of generosity, I bought a used $50 push mower for The Redhead's trim work. The Redhead got irritated with me when I presented it to her, and I remain convinced even now it was because she really wanted a tractor.

It was madness. This mowing consumed two days a week. You work five days, mow two, and then go back to work.

Well, as this summer approached, I started to feel bad for The Redhead. So I decided to bend my stubborn vow against yard work and do some mowing.

After about three hours, the bolts came loose and the motor fell off the riding mower. Two days later I got around to fixing it. The bolts were 43 cents, the wrenches, 43 dollars.

In the meantime, the lawn sort of got away from me. When I took the push mower out for trimming, it kept bogging down and killing. It only has a three horsepower engine, and those horses are awfully tired. So I went to *Link's True Value*, where they wait for me the way hawks perch on fence posts looking

20

for bunnies and bought The Redhead a new push mower and a string trimmer for Mother's Day.

Still, the yard remained an awesome chore.

I was thinking of calling for help. But as much as a guy loves having the in-laws around the house, I decided it wasn't fair to them.

Then, eureka! The idea hit like lightning. I would buy a tractor and a finishing mower—for The Redhead, of course. My friend Randy hooked me up with a guy in Minnesota who had a 1952 Ford 8-N tractor with a 6-foot hydraulic loader and a blade.

Naturally, this would have to be approved by my father-in-law. He's in charge of machinery at my house, and I am in charge of computers at his. Gary listened politely as I described my purchase.

"What do you need a loader for?" he wondered.

"To ahhh.... load stuff..."

"And why do you need a blade?"

I'm gonna blade my driveway," I told him.

"But your driveway is perfect," he sputtered.

"I can fix that," I assured him. I didn't mention my plans to get a snowblower and a post-hole digger.

A few days later, a truck went by my office with a tractor on the flatbed. "Hey, look everybody," I called, "Isn't that about the homeliest tractor you ever saw!?"

Then Randy got out of the truck.

"What do you think?" he said.

"It's yellow," I said. "Ford tractors are grey and red."

"Shhh," he said. *"It thinks it's a Minneapolis Moline."*

I was wearing bib overalls and a feed store hat when I went down to the implement dealer to order my 60-inch Farm King

21

mower.

While I was there, I looked at corn pickers. "Might put in corn this year," I announced loud enough for everyone at the parts counter to hear. "Then again, I might put half my acres into soybeans."

I sidled up to a farmer at the counter. He was getting filters.

"Whatcha runnin'?" I wondered.

"8970 New Holland. Got a real impressive PTO torque rise."

I puffed up my chest till it was almost even with my belly. "Runnin' an 8N Ford, myself," I bragged. "It's yellow."

He gave me the sort of look I expect deranged postal workers get and moved over to the next stool.

I've been testing the tractor for The Redhead, and it runs good. But the first day the belt started smoking until we jammed a broomstick behind the generator. Yesterday, I might have been running a little fast over the badger holes because the muffler fell off and got wedged under the mower.

I burnt my hand trying to pull it out.

I went in to get help and to explain to The Redhead, who was watching Dylan take a bath, that I had just mowed part of the tractor. We couldn't very well leave Dylan unattended, so a very naked three-year-old drip-dried in the fading evening sun as The Redhead, using potholders, pulled the muffler out while I lifted the mower.

She was pretty irritated.

She hates it when I break her stuff.

© Tony Bender, 2000

Jukebox Blues

There are smarter guys than me. And lots of guys handier around the house than I am. I'll admit that. Basic survival skills? I have none.

Let's just say this Y2K thing shuts everything down. Anarchy. No electricity. Rioting in Ashley over prune kuchen. Long lines for sausage in Wishek. Schnapps being rationed in Lehr.

Every man for himself.

Around here there will be guys making generators from old combine carburetors, a Slinky and baling twine.

I'll be eaten by wild dogs the first day.

I depend on specialists. You want a car fixed? Call a mechanic. Need a new deck on your house? Call a contractor. Need a large bulky object maneuvered down a narrow staircase without causing grievous structural damage to a dwelling?

Don't call me.

In fact, don't even let me pick the guy to call. Faced with moving a jukebox into the house in December, I was flummoxed. It's not like there's a listing under *Jukebox Movers* in the Yellow Pages. So I called our neighbor. He's a music teacher. It seemed like a good idea at the time.

But before we get to the part about his critical injury and the part where we destroy a goodly portion of the house and the divorce papers and the blood and all that, I should explain how

I got into this situation in the first place.

You see, my lovely estranged wife, The Redhead, chose the perfect gift for me for Christmas. An old jukebox. She wanted me to pick it out so we drove to Eureka one Sunday night to see a guy named Wolfgang.

I'm not making this up.

There in Wolfgang's shop was the exact model of the Seeburg jukebox they had in the Ponderosa Bar in Frederick, SD, almost 30 years ago.

I had to have the jukebox. But, I advised Wolfgang, I wanted it delivered to my basement. We probably wouldn't get it before Christmas, he said. So I was surprised when he showed up at the office the next day to announce he'd just delivered the jukebox. He'd left it outside by the front door. He didn't want to go in the house if no one was home, he said.

"You could have called," I grumbled. The problem was, I was on a tight schedule. After work, I had a job in the print plant. I sure as heck didn't want my precious jukebox sitting outside in -20 degree weather where it could be ruined or stolen. (At that point I didn't realize that theft was improbable since the jukebox weighs slightly more than the Queen Mary.)

So I got on the hotline to call the strongest guys I knew. No one answered. Then one of the ladies in the office suggested Allen, my neighbor. He had a Christmas concert to conduct that evening, but he agreed to come over for a few minutes.

Now, Allen isn't the biggest guy in the world. I mean, how bulked up can you get toting flutes and clarinets around? But I was grateful for his help.

We barely got the jukebox lifted into the foyer. The floor creaked ominously despite the fact that it had been reinforced prior to the installation of ceramic tile last fall.

In retrospect, I should have just let the jukebox crash through the floor to the basement from where it stood. It probably wouldn't have hurt the jukebox any, and the repair bill would have been cheaper.

But, I had help, I rationalized. Might as well do the job now. Allen insisted that he go first. We argued a bit before he reminded me that he was a music teacher and therefore most qualified to make that decision.

I heard the first tiles crack as we headed it down the narrow stairwell. Clay chips flew. Then more tiles shattered.

I'd like to tell you about the destruction, the wails of anguish, the pending litigation, and why Allen will never be able to hold a trombone in his mangled hands again, but this is a family column.

After the air ambulance whisked Allen away, I dialed The Redhead. The good news, I told her, was the jukebox had arrived before Christmas.

"What's the bad news?" she asked.

"Well, most of the tiles on the stairs are destroyed, and Allen may be dead."

"How bad are the tiles?" she asked.

The Redhead then informed me that my decision-making abilities were suspect (not in those words exactly) and that a bonehead and a music teacher have no business trying to move a 54-ton jukebox without adult supervision.

"I realized that once the jukebox headed down the stairs," I explained. "And, God willing, when Allen comes out of the coma, I think he'll agree."

I didn't really think it was fair that I was getting chewed out. After all, I had confessed. In the movies, when the spy spills his guts, the torture always stops.

I realized that The Redhead would be irritated at having a gaping hole where the stairs used to be—especially with the family coming on Christmas Day. But I'm not one to compound mistakes. I didn't try to fix it myself. I called our contractor, Bill. We call him that because he sends us a lot of them.

"You realize tomorrow is Christmas Eve," he advised me.

"I know, but I'll be a dead man by New Year's," I whimpered.

So on Christmas Eve, Bill sent a man to fix the stairs.

The jukebox sounds good. And other than its propensity for repeating *Layla* over and over, it works well for a jukebox that has endured 30 years of kicks from drunken cowboys.

I think when Allen gets out of intensive care, I'll bring him over to listen to it. And when Allen's better, Wolfgang must pay.

© Tony Bender, 1999

Gonna Have to Paint That

The painting I gave Grandpa for Christmas that year tells a tale that runs deeper than the canvas and the oils.

The painting depicts the first confrontation, out on the dusty prairies, of horses, horsemen and a smoke-belching, popping Model A in the early part of the century. The horses rear and snort wildly, nostrils flared, as riders struggle to control them.

Grandpa was the last of the cowboys, and this was a scene he had lived. He hung the painting crookedly in a place of honor in his living room. But it would look straight from his position sprawled out on the couch, he explained when I protested.

I did not tell him where I got the painting.

I didn't know the old man painted when I sought him out in the Badlands of North Dakota, but I knew he was an artist. He had been inducted into an old time fiddlers hall of fame, and I came to hear him play.

It was presumptuous of me to travel the back roads to that shotgun shack expecting a concert, but I was welcomed warmly with coffee in a sunlit kitchen with prehistoric appliances.

The fiddler was 82, yet he still was in demand at local summer festivals. He had picked up the bow when he was eight, and his playing had improved like fine wine.

He played a melancholy waltz and I was struck by his passion. His breathing became ragged and he struggled to hold back the tears. When he was done, my smile had to serve as the standing ovation I felt inside.

He sat and we talked and I asked about the paintings that hung on walls throughout the house.

They were like his children. Each with their own strengths and weaknesses. Flowers posed in vases and Vikings rowed and grimaced fiercely beneath shaggy beards. Cowboys rode the range. I thought about my grandfather and asked if the fiddler would sell one.

I didn't understand his hesitation.

He could surely paint more, I thought.

But the awful truth was he could not. He would sit in front of the canvas with brush in hand, but his muse had slipped away.

Dementia. The thief had stolen his visions.

It was his wife who told me that while the old man rummaged through the attic for a painting to sell.

Knowing what I knew, I didn't choose his best. But they were all good.

His only condition was that I photograph the painting so he would have something to remember it by. I assured him that the cowboys, horses and ancient motorist would have a good home. And my grandfather would relive his youth through another old man's hands.

I tucked the painting safely into my car, and we stood together in the warm autumn sun. A faded, unsteady grey fence separated the yard from a steep coulee where songbirds perched in dying branches.

The fiddler had his fiddle so I asked for an encore. He obliged and the music drifted from the strings across the plain.

The birds halted their song out of respect as the stiff, gnarled fingers worked the gut. I listened, enraptured, as the old man struggled to play as flawlessly as the birds had sung.

When he was done, he looked down at the birds, at the trees and at the rugged land below.

"I'm gonna have to paint that one of these days," he said.

What could I say?

I knew the scene would never be captured on canvas.

So I drank the picture in.

I memorized the deafening silence of the birds.

I listened to the wind in the dry grass, and I filed the old man's song in my memory.

And this morning I got up and I did what he could not do. I painted that scene on the canvas of a computer screen.

© Tony Bender, 1991

It Was a Good Thing

It was a good thing, really. The stubborn old Russian had always hated winter's dingy, bone-numbing cold. If he should cheat any season, it should be winter.

"What was he like?" the nurse gently asked after he had breathed his last, after she had smoothed the still-abundant grey hair on his head.

"He was a cowboy," the daughter answered, remembering the man.

Maybe I was just five or six, but I remember him, too, riding in some long-forgotten, dusty, prairie rodeo. Unusual, I think, for a grandfather several times over to be riding the broncs. But he was not a usual man.

The broncs left him with a metal plate in his leg, but he never got enough. He wouldn't ride the bulls though. "There's easier ways to die," he asserted. So he rode the untamed horses. And in his younger days, Harleys.

Five years ago, he hopped aboard my Suzuki, and we flew down the highway outside of Gackle, grinning at the wind-ripping acceleration.

When we pulled back into the yard, I turned sharply. "Never make it," he intoned. "No problem," I said.

When the 78-year-old and I had finished skidding on our asses across the grass, he helped me pick up the stalled machine, his eyes sparkling in amusement.

I was red-faced but he offered no admonishment.

That was the way he was.

It was the things he didn't say, I remember best.

Ten years before, we had raced snowmobiles over the bone-busting drifts, like madmen, to the end of the fence line. When I caught up, he grinned. And then we raced back, launching machines over three-foot drifts at 50 mph.

But he wouldn't ride the bulls...

That was before we lost Grandma, before the winters started to get longer and colder and bitter.

When the daughter called her brother in Washington, he was accepting. After all, John Spilloway had lived to be 83. Or was it 84? "If he didn't get it done in that time, well, then I guess he blew it!" the son said. And they laughed.

Yes, it was a good thing, they agreed.

When she called me, I had to ask about Chopper, Grandpa's 30-year-old quarterhorse. They were quite a pair in their day, those two. It seems every spring Chopper would dump the old Russian. And every spring, the old man would rise.

But now Chopper is thin and the spark is gone, and I wonder if he'll last the winter.

Spring won't be the same this year.

We talked for a long time, my mother and me. We laughed as we remembered the old Russian's good days.

But he had welcomed the end so when it came, well, yes, it was a good thing, we assured each other, with 300 miles of phone wires hiding the tears.

After the phone was nestled back in its cradle, I sat and mechanically began opening the day's mail in silence.

In a bright red envelope was a letter from my brother's wife and enclosed was a 5x7 of the latest member of the clan, crooked mouth goofily open, head tilted good naturedly, eyes shining.

One face steps out the door, and another steps in. That's the way it has always been, I told myself as I studied the face of my nephew. Yes, things are as they should be, I told myself.

And that's a good thing.

© Tony Bender, 1994

Chopper

The old quarter horse stood alone, sunning himself in the corral. His once strong back sagged under the weight of the years. Ribs poked through what was once a chestnut sheen.

I had a hard time believing it was him. He took a few steps closer to look me over. His eyes weren't much good anymore.

But as soon as he had satisfied himself that I wasn't a person of much importance, he creakily turned away, ancient but still arrogant.

"Hold on, old hoss," I called.

He stopped.

But you're not him.

"Nobody is," I replied. "But I needed to talk..."

So where is the old man?

"He won't be coming home, Chopper. He's a ghost rider now."

He gazed at me for a moment and then, like Grandpa would have done, he changed the subject.

I remember you now. You're the kid who used to feed me lemon drops.

"Sorry about that."

And then, just as quickly, the conversation shifted back.

So what's going to happen to me? I'm 30 years old...

I don't know for sure. Depends on who buys this place. If

the right family gets the place, they'll let you stay. If not, you'll probably go back to the old farmstead."

There was a man here last week, looking to buy a horse. Said I was a bag of bones. Said they should shoot me. They don't shoot horses, do they?

"Not you, Chopper. The old man would never have stood for it."

I miss him. I even miss the pipe smoke that made me sneeze. He was quite a man.

"Indeed."

I remember a trail ride in the Killdeer Mountains a few years ago. Heck, we were both getting old then, but we showed 'em.

The trail boss was no spring chicken himself. I remember one day he took a heckuva tough trail. Told everyone else to take the easy trail.

"Did you?"

Nah. The old man would have none of that. We followed the trail boss. We showed 'em.

The old man was a helluva rider.

"So why did you dump him every spring?"

Because I was a helluva horse.

And I think he would have been disappointed if I hadn't.

"I think you're right."

You know, I had a dream about him the other night. He was young and so was I. He had that mischievous twinkle in his eye, and I could run like the wind again. It was something, I tell you. It seemed so real... Can dreams be real?

"More real than this. They have to be. That's where the ghost riders live. It's that in-between place where we meet them. Yes, dreams are real, Chopper. I'm certain of it."

It's good we have dreams because nothing stays the same here. I never expected to get old... Look at those ponies out there. They just don't know...

And then, without a backward glance, his head bowed, he slowly and sadly walked away.

© Tony Bender, 1995

Writer's note: We had to have the vet put the big horse down the next year. His heart just wasn't in it anymore.

Back as a Butterfly

He'll be three this week, and my how our lives have changed in a thousand days. The first gurgle of a word has given way to actual conversation.

His moods still range from defiant to charming, but his ability to express them is more refined.

He and I were driving to Wishek the other day, and Dylan told me from the back seat, "Dad, we're out of gas!"

Naturally, I checked because this child constantly surprises us with his accurate assessment of situations.

"No, Dylan, we have plenty of gas," I assured him.

"Nope, we're out of gas, and we have to go to Willie's," he insisted.

Then I got it. When we fill up at Willie's Service, they always give Dylan a sucker.

Some days he's full of questions. Over a glass of chocolate milk, his brew of choice, he asked me *"What's this fork made of?"*

"Metal," I answered.

"What's the spoon made of?"

"Metal."

"What's my cup made of?"

"Plastic. But some are made of glass and some are made of metal."

This was getting tiresome. Then he hit me with a toughie.

"What am I made of?"

Hmmm. I knew it had something to do with puppy dog tails, but I guessed he wouldn't buy that.

"Well, you're made of bones and muscle and blood..." I struggled.

His brow furrowed as he listened. I could see I was losing my audience. Then, enlightenment.

"Dylan," I finished, "Mostly, you are made of love."

He smiled, a beatific, faraway look in his eyes, as he digested the thought. At times like that, there is no better job than being a father. There is no sweeter word than having your son call you, "Dad."

As parents, like all parents, we fret about our son's behavior. We are determined he will not be a rude, spoiled child. We are stubborn in our resolve and he, with a double dose of genetic parental stubbornness, is more than a match.

How we will fare, I do not know. But more important to me, is that he has a good heart. I don't know if that can be taught or if it simply *is* or *isn't*.

We shall try.

When I came home from work the other night, Dylan showed me his new pet, a caterpillar. The fuzzy creature was snug in a glass jar with plenty of green grass. The Redhead had put holes in the lid.

She told him how caterpillars eventually become butterflies or moths.

"What do you think he will become, Daddy?" she asked me as Dylan listened.

"A moth, probably," I responded. Sometimes I lack imagination.

By day two, we both had suggested that the caterpillar be

released. Dylan wasn't having any of that notion.

"But Dylan," his mother counseled, "If we don't let him go, he'll die." The caterpillar misses his mommy and daddy, she told him.

We lobbied gently for the caterpillar's release, but we left the decision to Dylan. The next morning before we headed to town, I suggested we release the bug.

"Yes, we're going to let him go," Dylan enthusiastically agreed. He carried the jar down the tiled steps, and I silently prayed he would not drop the jar and shatter the moment.

When we got outside, Dylan released the creature near the marigolds. Not satisfied when the bug didn't move, Dylan gently picked him up and moved him to the pavement.

The caterpillar needed no further prodding. It sprinted across the cement.

"When he comes back, he's going to be a butterfly," Dylan said. It was half question, half statement.

"Yes, Dylan," I agreed. "He's going to come back as a butterfly."

© Tony Bender, 1999

The Tigers Won Today

Hey Dad, the Tigers won today. Of course it was homers that saved the day for them again.

Tettleton hit another one. Can you believe the Orioles traded him away? Man, that just kills me. He's got 11 now.

I've been wanting to write to you for days now—ever since you left us—but I couldn't bear to tell you that the Tigers had lost. And they had. Every game since you've gone.

But hey Dad, they won today and they're still leading the American League East. Can you believe it? No pitching. No defense. Just home runs from Fielder, Tettleton, Deer and Gibson. How about Gibby's comeback? You gotta love it. He's really something.

Dad, I never really knew why you were such a Tiger fan. I never got the chance to ask. It was just one of those things that was. But it makes sense, a working class town. Tiger Stadium. Mickey Lolich. Al Kaline. Norm Cash. But of course he's gone now too. We're losing all our good Norms.

I have this picture in my mind of you walking off the baseball field in Ashley... You remember, the one north of the hospital. You were so young then and I was too, but I still remember that day. You were so skinny! You had a white T-shirt on and you carried that old style mitt. Mom was there, keeping an eye on me because I was so small.

I don't remember how you did that day. I was too young and I didn't understand The Game yet. But I'll bet you hit a homer. Yeah, I'm sure you did, Dad. You were really something.

Only one thing though... no matter how hard I try, I can't remember if you were wearing a Tiger hat. You must have been, but that part of my memory isn't clear. I was so young. You were so young.

It's funny, you were talking about baseball at the very end. Pastor Jeff told us. "Maybe we'll trade baseball cards in Heaven," he said to you. "Heck, maybe we'll *be* baseball players in Heaven." That's what he told us. Sad as it was we had to laugh a little. He was wearing a Mickey Mouse sweatshirt.

There's something wonderful about that. Talking baseball and praying in your final moments. Just like in the movies. It must have really been something.

Dad, I'm pretty sure you are playing baseball in Heaven. Hitting lots of homers.

You know, I've been an Orioles fan since Brooks and Boog but I want you to know that I'm cheering for the Tigers this year. It'd sure be something if Old Sparky could take 'em all the way, wouldn't it?

I'll be thinking about you if it happens. And I'll remember that day in Ashley. And I'll remember you hitting pop flies to me. I really miss that. And I really miss you, Dad. I love you, you know. You were really something.

By the way, Dad, did I tell you the Tigers won today....

Norman George Bender passed away on May 30, 1993. He was 55.

© Tony Bender, 1993

Boys of Summer

Every spring my hands long to grasp that perfectly imperfect ball with its red stitched seams and hourglass shaped leather strips.

Like a grizzly rising from a winter slumber, spring wakes up the boy in me who will always be 15 and roaming centerfields of grass and gopher holes.

I look at the black and white photo of that rag-tag championship team, and I am transported back. I can feel the sting of the bat as I foul off a fastball. And I feel the sting of the raspberry on my rump, but it doesn't hurt much. I was safe at the plate.

No one grows old in that picture. Not the deaf kid who played left field beside me—the kid who never heard the crack of the bat. And Kevin Hahn is still 5-4 and playing right field with his arm in a sling. When he makes a catch he flicks the ball to me, and I fire it to second base. And the runner is safe. Again.

While I'm there, Kevin gives me a handful of sunflower seeds from the bag he has stashed in his sling. On pitchers mound, Hawkeye patiently waits for us to complete the transaction. His black-rimmed glasses are still crookedly perched on his beak.

Our coach, Bob Fuhrman, stands beside me in that photo. He still wears that flannel work shirt and those lace-up work boots.

Moments before he had called me for a conference at the coach's box after I missed a pitch I should have drilled.

"Can you hit him?"

"I can hit him," I snap.

"Well, hit him then."

I do, and we win, but is any other outcome possible? Things never change in that black and white world. Life is different in this living color universe. It is flawed and unpredictable.

In that world, when I attempt the dramatic throw to the plate, the runners advance, and Bob still wants to know "What the heck did you go and do that for?" And because things never change in that world, I still don't know.

I write about that time, that place, because there's no one around to reminisce with anymore, and the deaf kid isn't listening. Once in a while, my brother will humor me and recount the home run I hit over the scoreboard in Ellendale. He was 9 or 10 then. His world was an immense place where big brothers did heroic things.

I remember the blast well—better than he does. It went foul. But in my brother's memory it is still a four-bagger, so I won't try to change his memory. It is flawed in a wonderful way.

And me, I have my own little black and white world framed and filled with kids with broken arms and crooked glasses. It is a place where we almost always win.

And when Bob asks me if I can hit the big fireballer, I know I can.

And Bob knows it too.

© Tony Bender, 1992

42

A Tale of Redemption

I remember the moment 20 years ago. I remember, not because I saw Muhammad Ali shock the world when he knocked out the impenetrable, undefeated George Foreman.

I remember because there was so much of me wrapped up in Ali back in 1974. The fights weren't televised then, and as a sophomore in high school, a ticket to Zaire was a little out of reach.

I had loved the Louisville Lip, his poems, his artistry. But then, when he emerged from government-imposed retirement, Joe Frazier proved Ali was, if not a mortal man, perhaps a lesser god.

Lord, Frazier was a machine. A left-hooking, unstoppable machine. I stood with him at the railing of a Missouri riverboat four years ago, and couldn't help but marvel at the man who would have been the greatest of his time if it had not been for The Greatest.

But the Great Frazier had fallen six times to the punishing fists of Bad George Foreman. Six times before ten minutes had passed.

So when Ali faced Foreman, I feared for Ali's life more than his reputation. But he was irrepressible, mocking Bad George's long looping punches. "He's tooooo slow," Ali said. Ali *knew* he could win. I hoped for survival first and held out with a glimmer of hope for a miracle.

That was the night, the sweltering evening, of the Rope-a-Dope. Ali broke all the rules. He let the jackhammer blows rain down until it could rain no more and then he felled the unbeatable Foreman. It was the crowning moment in Ali's life, cementing his claim as The Greatest.

And Bad George was never the same.

But time has a way of softening the raw edges of villains. It has a way of making mortal our lesser gods.

Fast-forward to November, 1994. George has become Curious George, Good George, and he's 45.

And he's even slower.

Ali, the butterfly, is so much older now.

Somehow a 45-year-old part-time preacher has talked his way into a shot at the title he left behind on the canvas in Zaire.

The new champ is Michael Moorer. I remember sitting a couple rows away from the glowering Moorer at a press conference after a Virgil Hill fight. "You don't want to fight this man, Virgil," I remember thinking to myself.

And here was Moorer, undefeated, facing a 45-year-old man in search of more than a belt. Good George was seeking some salve to soothe the disgrace two decades old.

Before the fight I was on the road with The Redhead, and I drove fast to get home. Things have changed. Championship fights are on television now.

As we settled down, I realized I was nervous, as anxious as I had been 20 years earlier.

But today I would exhort George.

Curious.

He was agonizingly slow, and he was battered early and often. Echoing Ali, the announcers decried his ponderous punches, his age, the false legend of his power.

"Knock him on his butt just once," The Redhead, not a notorious fight fan, urged. But she knew, I knew, the announcers and George knew, it would take a miracle punch.

But funny thing, miracles, sometimes they come when you hope for them. And funnier still, even then they surprise you.

In the tenth round, as Moorer lay supine, Preacher George knelt in the corner, praying, wearing the trunks he had worn two decades earlier when he'd lost a piece of his soul.

He arose the champion.

For the middle-aged men in the world, Good George expanded their horizons. In a world where 33-year-old quarterbacks are ancient, being a forty-year-old ex-jock can be a harsh reality.

But the story is more than that.

It is the story of the bad becoming good.

It is a curious story.

It is the tale of redemption.

© Tony Bender, 1994

Where Sons Go to Rest

I sat on the boulder, a mile higher than I had been yesterday.

The morning sun shone, and the mountain meadow deep below the jagged rocks of LaCrosse Pass glowed with a deep green.

Bright yellow, white and crimson blooms stood resilient, as important as the towering peaks and ice blue glaciers in the distance.

And I reflected here in these Olympic Mountains. I exalted in the back-breaking climb, and I grieved for the reason we were here.

Collin had first climbed this pass when he was about 12, his father told me as we ascended. The boy had seen the forbidding route and fretted.

"Go on," my uncle had told him, "And if you get scared, we can turn around." The boy didn't turn around, and in the years to come he had become a man, a formidable mountain man, carrying fifty pound packs, looking for bears to wrestle, his fear a distant memory.

But now free-spirited Collin was a memory too. A plastic box of ashes in my pack. His father would have carried him, but the accident had taken his other son, too. And he carried Greg. He had been the oldest.

I searched for profound thoughts to speak to a man who was scattering his youngest son's ashes.

"It was good that you could bring him up here one more time." My words broke the silence like thunder and drove Allen down the trail to be alone in his pain. And the tears mixed with ashes and ran down the mountain to the sea.

Twenty minutes later I hitched up my pack that had become an extension of me and followed him down. I slipped my headphones on and hit the tape.

Pink Floyd. Collin had liked Pink Floyd. We walked a long way that day, and the downhill was worse than the climb, rocks bruising my already blistered feet, the decline pounding my creaky knees. David Gilmour's guitar making it surreal. For nearly two days we wouldn't see another soul, a testament to the difficulty of the route.

We had pushed hard because we had one more son to take home. Greg had loved the pristine clarity of the small mountain pool, Marmot Lake, and that was another long climb, another hard day away.

The weather had been kind, but we rushed on expecting rain to come any minute. When you've lost your only sons, you come to expect the rain.

The sun had moved across the sky to the west before we stopped, utterly spent. I had been so engrossed in shutting out the pain that my heart refused to skip when I met the bear. His black fur glistened majestically, muscles rippled powerfully. But he moved on casually, out of respect I suppose, for our mission.

On the third day we stood on the rugged peak above Marmot Lake and surveyed distant waters and forests in crystalline weather. This time I was silent as Greg was laid to rest.

After he had finished, Allen seemed more at peace. We had

done what we had set out to do, and all that remained now was to get home safely.

And when his misstep didn't send him careening hundreds of feet down the cliff, I took it as a sign that his luck was changing. Surely he deserved to have a good life in the remaining years. Surely, his wife, Folly, waiting alone in that silent house a hundred miles distant, deserved peace of mind, I thought.

Righting himself after his wobble, Allen intoned, "You wouldn't have had to go down after me. Not in any hurry, anyway." Our eyes caught each other like a fishing line snagged on submerged moss, but nothing else was said.

On the fourth day, as the flames flickered, and the smoke drove away black flies left by a passing herd of elk, we stared at the orange tongues licking the branches.

"Many fathers would do many things for their sons," I said over the low rumble of the nearby mountain stream. "But not many would do what you've done, Allen. You've been a good father."

And we talked about his sons, and it was easier to laugh about their adventures and idiosyncrasies. They had been accomplished outdoorsmen. They had been good boys. They had been fine men.

On the fifth day as we walked out of the forest, I had fallen behind, a victim of protesting muscles and tendons that shortened my gait. But before we crossed the bridge that would complete our fifty mile trek, Allen waited. When I limped up he shook my hand. "You did good, buddy," he said. "I couldn't have done it without you."

Once again, my mouth could not give voice to what I felt. My throat was thick. It had all been so very hard. I wasn't as strong as Collin and Greg had been.

I looked straight ahead through the blur in my eyes. "It was a good hike," I choked out after the pause.

And then we walked across the bridge together.

© Tony Bender, 1993

So Long, Biff

When it was over, Bob called me. He knew I'd want to know. Biff and I had a special bond. I'd saved his life twice, and he never forgot it.

The first time he was just a pup. Rose had brought him home from the pound, and when I stopped by, I heard him howling pathetically in the bathtub where he had been banished. It was the relentless wailing that had Rose to the breaking point. So frazzled was she that she was ready to take him back to the pound.

I peeked into the bathroom. He was a grey little bundle of psychoses. Truth be told, he had no distinguishable redeemable features. And as it turned out, he was an average dog, at best.

I lobbied Rose. "You can't take him back to the pound after you've saved his life."

"Someone else will adopt him," she rationalized.

"No way. Look at him. He's pathetic. If you take him back, he's a goner."

It was the truth and she knew it. Thus, Biff became a member of the Greenfield family. As good as Bob is with dogs, Biff retained his mysterious psychic scars. As he grew, his grey coat turned brown, and he started to resemble a coyote.

He never really warmed up to people as a rule. He'd hide under the coffee table and bark at strangers.

But for me, Biff always reserved a warm welcome.

Instinctively, he knew he owed me his life.

The second time I saved him was a bit more dramatic. I'd accompanied Bob and Rose to the mountains. Biff threw up on the way, like he always did.

It was spring and torrents of ice-cold water cascaded violently down the mountain. Bob and I started hopping from boulder to boulder, midstream, above a 50-foot waterfall. Biff followed. So did Chelsea, their other lummox of a dog.

But Chelsea's ungainly leap toppled poor Biff into the frigid water. The swirling current started to carry him away. But fortuitously, it brought him within arm's reach. I had one chance. I didn't miss. I pulled the shivering wretch to safety by the scruff of his neck.

After that, no matter how many years it had been, Biff always remembered. He'd sleep at my feet when I visited. Bob always marveled at the change in his anti-social dog when I was around.

In June, when I arrived for our annual fishing trip, both dogs looked creaky.

"Those dogs are getting old," I told Bob as I scratched Biff's ears. Biff was 12.

Last week, Biff got sick. There was a tumor above his spleen. It had burst. But the vet gave him a prescription that might give him a few more quality days.

So Bob and Biff got to play catch one more time. And to the end, Biff took advantage of his situation. He refused to eat anything but hamburger and candy.

Tuesday, Biff went outside and just lay down. Sad eyes. So Bob took him in. But not before feeding him one more candy bar.

And then he called me.

The conversation was pretty matter-of-fact. "I mentioned your name to him," Bob said. "I was going to call you, so he could hear your voice one more time."

Funny how guys can get sentimental about a dog.

Bob was about to hang up when I cut him off. "What kind of candy bar did you give him?" I wondered. It seemed important.

"A Twix," Bob replied. We both agreed that a Twix was a fine last meal for a dog. Then the Redhead came home with Dylan, and I shelved all thoughts of Biff.

But the next day I had a two and a half hour drive to Bismarck, and I started thinking about that old dog. We'd come a long way, Biff and I, from that bathroom off Mississippi Street.

Bob taught him all those tricks and kept him fed and groomed. But I always kind of felt that Biff was my dog. And I think Bob conceded that, too. I got a little sentimental thinking about Biff. I don't really know why. He was just an average dog.

Maybe it was because this time I couldn't do anything for him.

© Tony Bender, 1996

52

Little Man's Big Heart

It's easier to transplant a liver than a dog. That I've learned through experience. When we moved to rural Ashley 18 months ago, our Brittany, Duck Dog, refused to stay home and eventually, we think, ended up as coyote chow. We still miss the bonehead.

Last summer, a close friend, Tom Secrest, gave me a three-year-old German wire-hair. He breeds the dogs. We named the dog Law Man, an acknowledgement of Tom's profession as an attorney. Dylan, however, couldn't pronounce it. So this animal, the size of a Shetland pony, is inappropriately dubbed Little Man.

Dylan loves his Little Man and the dog is gentle with him. But he can put on a fearsome show when strangers arrive. He reminds me a lot of Secrest. Last fall, when we had friends drive in to celebrate my 40th birthday, Harriet Howe brought her dog along. Naturally, they tangled. Harriet rushed out to see how her dog had fared, half-believing he had won.

"C'mon," I said, bringing her to her senses, "What did you think would happen? That's Secrest's dog!" Harriet's dog ended up with a mangled ear and an $80 vet bill.

Little Man has a sociable side too. At least once a week, Little Man will make a break for LeMar Haas' place which is less than half a mile as the crow flies or the dog gallops. LeMar has lots of horses and cattle, but the big attraction for Little

Man is cattle dogs. One of the dogs, Magnum, is a grumpy, growly 15-year-old. I've seen him snap at Little Man many a time but Little Man never fights back. "He just takes it," LeMar marvels. I guess I understand Magnum's point of view. When you get old and creaky, youngsters can be downright annoying.

We have the routine down pretty well. I'll come home from work and The Redhead will report, "Little Man took off."

I might wait till after supper to get him. Or if it's too late, I might wait till morning. But when I drive over, Little Man loads up in the back of the Explorer like a naughty boy, and I haul him back home. Taxi service. I've never as much as raised my voice to him because he's such a sensitive dog. I guess we have this understanding.

LeMar has been real understanding, too. I think one of these days I'm going to attach a note to Little Man's collar and a kuchen to his tail. "You and Jeanne come for coffee," the note will read. "Please bring our dog."

Last weekend, Little Man made his jailbreak early Saturday morning. I waited until evening to fetch him, deciding to let him get in a long visit. He'd been acting a little weird. I heard him whining the night before in his doghouse. Though it was raining, he'd been through a lot tougher weather than that. But eventually, I went out and let him spend the night in the garage. He seemed upset about something.

When I pulled up to LeMar's, I couldn't see Little Man. Usually, he surrenders like a prisoner of war. LeMar's young dog was herding a wayward cow into the corral when I arrived—a thing of beauty to see a good cow dog work.

But no Little Man and no Magnum. LeMar walked me over to a plow on the far south end of his yard where Little Man jumped up and barked a warning.

LeMar explained. He wasn't sure if Magnum was just sick or dying, but Little Man had taken it upon himself to nursemaid the old dog. He had spent the day keeping Magnum warm in the cold spring drizzle. I have to admit to getting a little sentimental over LeMar's story.

Little Man cried the whole way home. When he unloaded, I roughed up his ears like I always do, and I pounded his ribs like a drum. He looked up at me with those sad brown eyes, and I held his head in my hands.

"Little Man," I told him, "You have a good heart."

© Tony Bender, 1999

Writer's note; A day or so later, old Magnum finally died. Little Man took it hard.

It Wasn't My Place

It was odd, I always thought, that my father should have been so attached to that cat. He didn't seem like the type. But the times I walked into the living room to see that orange monster curled up on Dad's belly as he stretched out on the couch, I can't begin to count them.

Scruffy was the offspring of Mom's beloved manx-angora cross and some anonymous, child support-skipping, alley cat Romeo. As you might have guessed, Scruffy wasn't a handsome kitten. He had no tail and his tongue protruded from between his fangs giving him a quizzical expression that suggested he was a few pecks short of a bushel.

But he grew up to be an impressive specimen, large and well-muscled, reminding me of a bobcat with paws the size of pot-holders. Only Dad would have dared roughhouse with Scruffy the way he did. And it seemed the more Dad ruffled his fur and tumbled him across the carpet, the more Scruffy adored him.

Sometimes, on a schedule akin to that of Halley's Comet, Scruffy would let someone else pet him. But more often than not, he would slap one of those massive paws on your hand, dig his claws ever-so-slightly into your skin and just dare you— *dare you*—to move. No one ever tried. Unless you wanted your hand transformed into hamburger, you waited until Scruffy, yawning and looking disinterested, granted you parole.

Scruffy ruled the neighborhood for years. Few were the felines *or canines* who dared trespass. But the battles took their toll. More than once, Scruffy tangled with two toms at once. Tattered ears and lumpy scars beneath tangled fur documented tales of fearsome exchanges.

But even tougher on Scruffy than those battles, was the loss of my father. In those final months when the hospital stays became a permanent absence, Scruffy mourned with us.

One day, a few weeks after the funeral, as I strode through the house, back for a weekend visit, I spied Scruffy lounging in the sun. Like a man with nothing to lose, I grabbed Scruffy by the neck like my father had done. I ruffled his fur until static made sparks fly. I gleefully bounced him across floor like a soccer ball. When he righted himself, Scruffy shook himself and looked at me, stunned. For a split-second, he must have thought his master had returned. "That was for Dad," I laughed.

But I never tried that again. It wasn't my place.

As the winters passed, Scruffy started to resemble his name more and more.

The neighborhood cats got tougher.

Scruffy got older.

He started losing catfights, coming home terribly mauled. As skinny as he became, his bravery remained undiminished, a warrior to the end. Each winter, I surveyed the damage and tsk, tsked, "It will be a sad day when Scruffy is gone."

Scruffy was a living connection to Dad.

When Jim came into our lives, married Mom and moved into the house, he fit like an old shoe. I'm sure it wasn't easy to live in what had been another man's home, but he made the transition with grace. Because it was what my mother wanted. And it just made sense. Her ceramics shop is next door.

Sometimes it's the little things, not grandiose gestures, that make you appreciate people, that give you a glimpse into their character.

I'm sure Jim understood very clearly Scruffy's connection to my father, and it would have been easy to be threatened by it—or at least put off by it. But Jim doted on that cat like a mother hen. He warmed milk—*microwaved it*—and fed Scruffy like royalty. He fretted when he didn't come home.

These kindnesses I observed with satisfaction.

Still, Scruffy got thinner and thinner. Last winter I was sure would be his last. But the last time we visited, he was still there to greet us on the sidewalk with a rub on a pant leg.

But this winter, whatever was eating him up inside finally got the best of him. A few weeks ago, Jim and Mom heard him howling in anguish in the garage.

So Jim picked up his rifle and delivered the final kindness.

I could not have done it.

It wasn't my place.

© Tony Bender, 1999

Dreams For Sale

Dreams for sale. Those are my dreams for sale today, mister.

You know, when I called the auctioneer, this day seemed so far away. I stalled for days before I called.

It's hard selling your dreams.

I remember so well the day we bought this place. I remember like a proud papa the day we bought that Versatile. It's all been years ago, but inside I still feel like that young man who built this farm.

But when I look in the mirror, I see the years.

I didn't sleep much last night. I worried that the weather would be bad, that things wouldn't sell well. And I was half afraid that things *would sell* at all.

But there's no turning back.

The neighbors are here and so are relatives from far and wide. It's like a funeral except brown Key coveralls and six-buckle overshoes are uniform of the day. But nobody died. And 300 strangers won't come to my funeral.

Move along, folks.

Nothing to see here.

Man's just selling his dreams.

We didn't miss the dairy herd when we sold it a year ago. They kept us from a thousand functions and now there is more time for kids and grandkids. Man, they grow up fast.

But the finality of selling those tractors and all that haying equipment is starting to sink in. Of course, no one can tell except my wife. She's the one who wears her heart on her sleeve today. Her eyes are red and her voice hoarse. Says she's got a cold. But I think she's going to miss that old grain truck. Sure, it smokes to beat the band, and the passenger side door flies open on left turns like a wounded duck trying to soar, but that truck is like a homely sister. You love her just the same.

But don't judge the quality of my equipment by that truck, mister. I took care of my machines. They were shedded and serviced regularly. I didn't take care of myself nearly as well.

I know it might sound a little weird, but I feel like I'm sending puppies to strangers. I want my machines to have a good home.

It's gotten to the point of embarrassment the way the auctioneer keeps bragging up my equipment. He calls me a proud man. A man who took pride in keeping up his equipment. But it's the God's-honest-truth. I even hauled that Versatile in to the shop last week just to make sure it was 100 percent perfect; even though, I knew it was. I don't want anyone to feel cheated.

Man's reputation is something sacred.

The auctioneer was optimistic the day we signed the contract. Said it should be a barn-burner of a sale. But today he backed off of his prediction a little. But we'll just have to see what happens.

Besides, when a guy's selling his dreams... well... ain't no price you can put on that.

As I watch the men slog through the mud today, I know I'm doing the right thing. The time is right. Weather's been uncooperative the last couple years. Too wet. Cattle price iffy. And milk prices? Don't even want to talk about it.

It's not like it used to be. It's not automatic. Sons don't take over the farm much anymore. The dream business has changed.

But when I see young farmers in spirited bidding for my equipment, it makes me feel good. They're counting the hours saved if they can put two seed drills in the field come snow melt. That swather is a bargain and Junior ought to be able to handle it by June.

That's the way I was. Seemed like I had a year-round sunburn on my neck. Gosh, those were the days. We were quite a team, me and the wife. We had rhythm that was a beautiful thing at harvest. She'd haul one truck to the elevator, and I'd be topping off another when she pulled back into the field. Pert' near always in step. Like Fred and Ginger of the spring wheat.

Now, the dance belongs to the bidders. They look at each other across the crowd, a cross between gunslingers and bashful beaus at their first dance. As the bid escalates, the auctioneer points at them both.

Wanna dance?

Heads nod imperceptibly. Fingers twitch. Eventually, one of them looks at his shoes and wanders away. Guess the old corn head will do for another year.

The auctioneer is glib. When he pitches those five feed bunks, everyone knows two have seen better days. But he gamely marches on, his cadence rat-a-tat-tatting like Gene Krupa. "C'mon boys, them cows don't know the difference between a good one and a broke one. Go ahead and buy 'em. Fool them cows!" The last two go for $30. They'll make a fine bonfire some day.

After the sale, the auctioneer is beaming. It's been a good sale. He was right all along—the first time. The church ladies have had a big day as well, selling $2 hot dogs and $3 burgers and potato salad advertised on every sign with Dan Quayle's extra e. Lotta Republicans here today, but I suppose their money's as good as the next guy's.

Well, nice talkin' to you, mister. But I gotta go now. The guy who bought the 2+2, wants me to pull it into the shed for the night. Lotta room in there today.

I know my wife will be watching from the kitchen as I drive it for the last time. Tonight, when we're finally alone, that's when we'll talk, and we'll assure each other that selling our dreams today was the right thing to do.

Now, I ain't no poet. But any farmer worth a damn stops once in a while to watch the sun rise and see the poetry around him. I'll try to express what's on my mind to her tonight. I guess I want her to know that while we sold our dreams today, we're keeping the memories.

Good memories.

© Tony Bender, 1998

The Best Gift

The young girl would sift, fascinated, through her grandmother's jewelry box. They were not the crown jewels, mind you. On hard-scrabble North Dakota farms in those days, precious dollars went toward equipment and basic necessities.

Still, the sparkling baubles, housed in a nondescript jewelry box on a simple dresser, in the tiny home beneath the majestic weeping willow, were treasures in the granddaughter's eyes.

There was a story behind each piece. A tale to be told. And the young girl never tired of handling the necklaces, earrings, bracelets and rings. And she never tired of hearing the stories.

It was the simple gold band with the diamond that held the best secret, and the young girl never forgot. She shared the tale along the way.

That's where I heard the story. But there was never a happy ending. The ring was destined to leave the farm. Grandmother had said so, long ago. This caused no small amount of consternation to the young girl who knew...just knew...her very own mother deserved the ring. But gifts do not always go to the most deserving.

Sometimes we look past those around us. It's human nature. We surround ourselves with the ones we love. And then we take them for granted. The flaws, the quirks, the moles; they irritate beyond reason. But we are an impatient lot, those of us on

Schoolhouse Earth.

Maybe that's what happened between the grandmother and her own daughter—the one who raised the young girl just across the driveway in the very same farmyard just 70 yards from that grand old weeping willow.

Maybe the grandmother just lost sight and measure of the kindnesses that came her way. Or maybe, like so many of that generation, hard times had forced clenched teeth and stiff upper lips. A stoicism that masked too much. A stoicism that would not allow a thank-you. Because that would create a crack in the facade, and the whole wall might crumble.

The grandmother had held the engagement ring precious for so very long now. It was the same one her mother had worn.

The ring had been intended for another hand. But all things, all people, have a destiny, and destinies are not subject to the plans and minor whims of the students here on Schoolhouse Earth.

Two beaus stared at the cards that night. The aces, queens and kings, now long forgot. One man had lost too much and now, all that separated him from his shirt was the ring intended for the hand of his sweetheart.

I don't know if the unlucky gambler's sweetheart ever got a ring. Or if they were ever married. If they ever had little, inquisitive, redheaded, freckled great-grandchildren. I do know his sweetheart never got that particular ring.

The other beau in this roguish lot also had a sweetheart and that ring went home in the pocket of the man with the better cards. And years later his daughter told the tale of the ring's journey to the gambler's great-granddaughter in that tiny house beneath the weeping willow.

Perhaps the ring knew it's destiny all along. But we did not know, and every time the young girl told the story, it always ended with a sad question mark. She did not know if the ring's journey would take the turn she felt it should. She understood that destinies such as these are not ours to direct. But you can't help but think about it.

You learn to accept things as you grow, and the young girl had learned well the lessons of acceptance that come with marriage and motherhood.

I was there when the gift was opened. I was sitting between them when Grandmother's daughter opened the small box. I heard the quiver in her voice as she asked across the din of noisy toys and crackling paper, "Are you sure you want to give this to me?"

Grandmother nodded, but I'm still not sure if she really heard the question. The years have claimed so much of her hearing. She sat, stoic as ever, but she looked satisfied. It was a wonderful gift. It was a wonderful gift because it said so many things that will probably always be unsaid.

The young girl beamed at her mother's gift, and she told the story about the ring's shady past, again, to another audience.

"It was the best gift of all," the young girl told me that night as we drove under crisp, twinkling winter stars, our son sound asleep, still clutching favorite Christmas toys.

© Tony Bender, 2000

Laughter Stolen

S he would have been a July baby. I say *she*, because I was so sure it was going to be the little girl we wanted to add to the family. We had names picked out for a girl and a boy. And another boy would have been just dandy.

Julie and I didn't tell anyone about the pregnancy. We didn't say a word the last time until she was six months along. So we talked, just us two, about how silly it was that we had eliminated a bedroom just this summer. We talked about adding on. We fretted about money.

We wondered how Dylan would react. His Mom told him about the baby in her tummy and he was enthralled. He asked about it daily. And he listened intently to the tale of his own birth.

We hadn't seen her yet, but this little girl was already having a big impact on our little family.

The day Julie told me she thought there was something wrong, I filed it away. She had worried her way through the first pregnancy, and it had turned out just fine, hadn't it? But the next day we agreed she needed to call the clinic in Aberdeen. It sounded like a miscarriage, they said, not meaning to be unsympathetic but sounding that way just the same. If it was a miscarriage, there was really nothing they could do, they said.

You can't stop it. Come in when you can.

The season's first blizzard stranded us at home for the next two days, waiting. We couldn't chance a trip on icy roads with Dylan. And if we got stranded, he would have been stuck at day care. So we waited. Knowing the answer. Still hoping we were wrong.

I hadn't allowed myself to think about how I would feel. But when Julie walked out of the examining room, I could see the loss in her eyes. She waited till we were in the car to tell me the news.

And in a wintery parking lot we wept.

My sorrow surprised me. I thought about the times I dismissed the news of a miscarriage. I never recognized the loss of the hopes and dreams a parent has for a child.

Clarity slices like a blade through me now.

We hadn't shared the excitement of the pregnancy, so it was difficult to share our loss. But we told our parents and closest friends. One sage friend says it's a loss society doesn't recognize.

If you lose a loved one, there is a face. There are memories. We did not know our child's face, her laughter, her strengths and weaknesses. We did not get to brush tangles from her hair, to fret past midnight on her first prom night. Her laughter has been stolen from us.

That is why we silently grieve. It is why we sometimes get a faraway look in our eyes. It is why we hug each other and Dylan tighter than before. That is why we savor the laughter in our lives so much more. That is why we smile at your children.

Last week, as I ordered at the lunch counter, the ladies hovered around the newest baby, just a couple weeks old. I had to get closer.

Such a beautiful little girl. Such a beautiful child.

Sometimes it seems so easy.

As I wrote this column, music on the stereo, Dylan burst into the room. "Let's dance Daddy! Daddy, let's dance!"

I started to tell him that I needed to finish my work, but I caught myself. So we danced. We danced our silly dance and grinned at each other. We're very good dancers.

We must always make time for dancing.

© Tony Bender, 1999

A Mother's Tears

When tragedy appears at the editor's desk, we become proficient at looking the other way. Lock up the emotions. Just do the story.

Sometimes that dam springs a leak.

She came into our office last week with heavy baggage, her son's obituary and photograph. Every week, a spouse, a brother or sister, offers with trembling hands, the obituary that falls so short of encapsulating a life.

But there is nothing so heavy as a mother's sorrow.

The ladies in the office admired the handsome young man in Navy dress whites.

"He looks like Tom Cruise," I said.

"He got a little tired of hearing that," his mother said, a wry smile creasing her face. I repeated my condolences and retreated to my office. Behind the wall.

There is nothing so sad as a mother's tears.

I couldn't get it out of my mind. There is nothing so obscene as a parent outliving a child. I thought of my uncle and aunt who had lost both sons on one tragic day a few years ago. The young men had attempted to recapture a piece of their boyhood by climbing a tree. They'd fallen to their deaths.

I remembered that gut-wrenching hike as my uncle and I carried his sons' ashes into the Olympic Mountains where they loved to hike.

It was an exorcism of grief. A goodbye that had been otherwise denied them.

And I remembered my own father lying on his deathbed, his father at his side. Time reversed itself. My father appeared to me as a scared little boy. My grandfather grew decades younger, though still weighted down by the sorrows of age. And like any father would tell a son, he said, "You just do the best you can, Norman."

One grieving mother brought those memories flooding back.

These were the thoughts that stomped, then whispered, then stomped again through my mind.

I had just dried Dylan off from his evening bath, and he perched on my knee, watching his mother prepare supper.

I started to tell her about the grieving mother. About what an exceptional young man he must have been.

But out of nowhere, the wall began to crumble.

I spoke.

I stopped.

I tried again.

Dylan stopped fidgeting. Julie peered, questioningly, out from under the cabinets.

I looked away, embarrassed.

I gazed at Dyan, freshly polished, wide-eyed and curious, smelling sweetly of baby lotion.

I could not continue.

© Tony Bender, 1997

You Just Move On

North Dakota can give you a lot of things. Peace of mind. Here you can still sleep at night with the door unlocked. Nobody steals the Sunday paper off the stoop. In the bastard winters you can keep the car running at the gas station while you go inside.

And North Dakota's sons are legend. Hard working, no-nonsense farm boys. Boys with heart. They'll come to work with a cold and do twice the work of your average city boy. Got a tough job? *Hey, you, Dakota Boy. Come here.*

Yes, North Dakota can give you a lot. It can also get you walking point your very first day in Vietnam when you're 20.

Where are you from?

"You can count on walking point from now on," Don Davidson's platoon leader said after hearing the answer. North Dakota boys were just more aware.

You could trust them.

That was the word.

Davidson didn't sleep that night. But just a few months removed from the Dakota plains, how could you sleep? Certainly not after that frantic, tree-top-skimming helicopter ride at break-neck speed from Duc Pho. And when the chopper landed at the clearing, they pointed you in the right direction. You ran faster than you'd ever run before, half expecting to take a bullet in the next second.

And now, in the morning it would be your job to walk point. Your job to detect the mines—to either find the trail around them or to set them off with your own foot.

Point man walked alone.

It was your job to sniff out the ambush. The Viet Cong would let the point man pass and then open up on the rest of the platoon. Welcome to Danang. "You were scared for yourself...Scared you were going to screw up and everyone else was going to suffer."

There was plenty of pain to go around in June of 1968. Of the 20 men Davidson came to Vietnam with, including the eight who were assigned to his platoon, three went home in one piece. There was William LaBarbera from Chicago, Kent Weinberger from Redig, California and Davidson.

Good friends.

Close friends.

But when you get home you don't call them. Like the kids from summer camp you've forgotten, you never call. You never write. That would mean remembering. "That's how I deal with it," says Davidson. "I don't."

You just move on.

LaBarbera, who lives in Elmwood, IL now, was with Davidson the day he got his first Purple Heart. The Viet Cong had an American Special Forces unit surrounded. Davidson and LaBarbera were perched on a hill, watching friendly air strikes try to save them when an enemy mortar landed in front of them. Davidson wound up with a piece of shrapnel sticking between his eyes. "It was sticking out half an inch," LaBarbera remembers. "He said, 'Pull it out.' But I said, "No, you've got to go back."

Davidson went back for treatment while LaBarbera, who

never got more than jungle rot in Vietnam, cussed the lucky son of a gun. Davidson was sure to get a week off, he thought.

An hour later the helicopter returned with supplies.

Davidson was aboard.

He was one of the guys you could count on. You learned to tell from the first moment who you could trust when it got deep. You learned who you couldn't. "You could almost tell from the very first moment you saw them," Davidson remembers. "Some absolutely couldn't hack it. They had to be pulled out."

It was insane. Anything could happen. You could only see a few feet ahead in the tangled jungle. Hell, you might walk right into a VC camp.

It happened.

"Absolutely walked right into their camp. Just like that." He snaps his fingers for effect. "Instant chaos."

"You always thought you were on top of everything." But anything could happen. At any moment. No, you had to be more than good.

You had to be lucky.

Lucky, like the time Davidson called a meeting of platoon leaders. On this day, as they met beside a boulder, Davidson idly toed the pack of Marlboros lying by the rock. He might have picked them up on another day to claim the remaining few cigarettes. But today, he just nudged the pack with his boot. Nudge. Nudge. Then he saw the wire...

No, you had to be lucky.

In the final days you thought about going home. But you couldn't count on it. A month before he was scheduled to go home, Davidson found himself in a major battle. Of the 990 Americans who went in, 20 came back in one piece.

If your eyes could be opened any wider, they were. "What a

beautiful country it could be without a war," he remembers thinking.

Davidson came home with two Purple Hearts, a Bronze Star and a Distinguished Service Cross. When he returned, Davidson had just turned 21, but he'd grown up more than the numbers could measure. Like soldiers in a hundred wars before, he'd loaded up the bodies of fallen comrades, trying not to feel. "You just kind of got mechanical about that sort of thing," he says."You just move on."

Twenty-one years after the war's end, he breaks his silence.

He stirs the memories.

Scratches at the scabs.

Examines the scars.

Enough time has passed. "It was long enough ago," he says. "I just never dealt with it. I just always had my mind set on something else."

Anything else.

North Dakota can give you a lot of things.

Distance.

Family. Elaine and children, Jill and Troy.

He's moved on.

The framed medals suggest he's a hero. He dismisses the notion in a split second. "There were as many heroes as there were guys over there," he says.

That said, he moves on.

© Tony Bender, 1995

Bill's Story

The worst of it was not ever having any rest. Never a night's sleep. They were always cold, always wet. Always scared. That's what The Redhead's great uncle Bill told me as we leaned on his car outside the big shed at the family reunion.

When she introduced him, The Redhead mentioned Bill had landed at Utah Beach on D-Day. Bill jumped in on cue and cursed the war—any war. All wars. "But I was lucky; came home without a scratch." The family was lucky. Five sons went to war. Five returned.

Bill was in his mid-20s when he ducked German bullets in slit trenches as a member of Omar Bradley's 1st Army. In peacetime, Bill had volunteered "but they classified me as 4-F." But when war broke out, "I was 1-A," he says.

As he talked, and as I listened, we surveyed the tots swinging on swings and sliding on slides in the sunshine. Then Bill continued. He didn't need much prodding. His voice boomed, the voice of an artillery man, out of sync with his frail body.

Sure, Utah Beach was no picnic, but them boys over on Omaha Beach, now they had hell to pay, Bill said. The bombers hadn't been able to knock out the German big guns and machine guns on the cliffs. Landing crafts were blown up in the water. Bodies littered the shore. And if you made it to the beach, there were only cruel choices. You could stay there and die or rush the hail of machine gun bullets. It was enough to tick anyone off. It made you mad enough to kill.

From there it was extended misery. The cold. The sogginess. No rest. That's what struck Bill the most. A year of lying sleeplessly in mud with shells whizzing overhead. Think there's glory in war? PFC Bill Crystal didn't see any. Patton, now he got accolades. "I never understood why he got all the press," Bill complains. "We were right there beside him all the time."

Bill was there for the Battle of the Bulge, the last gasp gamble by a desperate German army. They almost pulled it off, but when the Germans were pushed back, it was just a matter of time.

And Bill was there at Leipzig, giving Hitler hell with five-inch, hundred-pound shells. "The last shots fired in Europe were on Leipzig, you know."

One day, the water truck came by and dropped off four jerry cans. Then the message came across the radio. The war was over. Bill and the boys slumped in relief, but the sergeant was having none of that. He ordered the men to clean up the cannon. Bill roars at the notion. "Clean up the cannon! We didn't give a damn if that thing ever fired another shot. We were all out at the end. There was nothing left."

Then someone opened one of the jerry cans. It was filled with beer. So were the others. "We got drunker than snot," Bill says. "Boy, did we get drunk."

© Tony Bender, 1998

The Viking

When I was a boy, all my paths led to The River. But it was years before I learned its name. I grew up thinking it was the James, but in reality it was the Maple. A Sioux tribe, led by a now obscure chief, had camped at its shores long ago.

I learned to swim in that river but not well enough to beat Annie Oschner. And it was from those waters that my friend Gare Bear—the best floater of us all—emerged wailing, glistening with leaches. We salted him down until he looked like Lot's wife. He hadn't known leaches love coconut oil.

Yet, there was peace at the river, and I often found myself gazing at the reflection of the pines on the opposite shore. I would think boyishly-grand thoughts and watch the huge old snapping turtle break the shimmering glass surface. I wondered if Sioux boys had watched him a century ago, before his shell was the size of a '64 Chevy hubcap.

With a roll of kite string, a hook and a piece of tin foil I would victimize bullheads. And if they weren't biting on shiny objects, I would wade in the muck until I found a clam to be sacrificed on the concrete of the dam and cut up for bait with my Barlow jackknife.

If even that failed, I would sing *Let the Sunshine In* to lure the fish. It worked. I swear to God, it worked. Me and the Fifth Dimension, catching fish.

That's how I spent my days. Fishing. Singing. Thinking. Watching ancient reptiles. Discovering answers for questions I hadn't yet learned.

One day when I got to the river I saw *him*. He was old, wrinkled and calmly watching a red and white bobber in the middle of the stream. He was fishing on the north side of the dam. Hell, I'd never seen *anyone* catch anything there-except leaches—and *you* had to be the bait. But there he was, looking to all the world, like a fisherman. He looked so sure of himself I couldn't help but draw closer.

I still thought it was folly. I mean, fishing on that side of the dam was crazy. Crazier even than singing to fish on the south side. I sat with him, hypnotized by the float drifting in the breeze. I really wasn't a believer, but he was doing what all Norsemen must do, challenging the water and the creatures below. The bobber never moved that day, but I couldn't help myself. I went back the next day, and he was there with two rods.

So we sat, the calm certain old Viking and me, the unbeliever, the minstrel to fish. We didn't talk. We couldn't. He didn't speak English, not uncommon in a community of old Finlanders. And the only words I knew in Finn were swear words. I was fluently foul in two languages.

With gnarled, patient hands he taught me knots and the right way to bait a hook, and he grinned with yellowed teeth when I started to catch on. We fished perfectly to no applause, no clapping fins.

And so it went on. I stopped thinking about catching a fish— the rods seemed to be an afterthought, a part of a ritual begun so long ago it had lost its meaning.

The days ran together, the script never changing, until the

afternoon my bobber jerked below the surface and the reel started screeching. I couldn't have been more stunned if the Loch Ness Monster had surfaced in my bathtub.

Grabbing the rod, I strained as the pole bowed downward and the Viking excitedly shouted useless Finnish instructions to my English ears. I played the fish badly, yet in spite of myself, managed to land a healthy five pound northern pike—the first of my life.

I grinned. He grinned. We both grinned until our faces hurt. And then we grinned some more. My God, it was a miracle! A blessed event.

You know, when you're young and green, you don't realize when a memory has been formed. You don't know that some inspired master in that dark mysterious world of self has carefully packaged the moment and stored it lovingly away.

It appears on its own with no warning—like the fish—and it never tarnishes. It comes back gleaming. That is what I remember.

I recall, too, the day I waited at the river and the Viking didn't show. I found out later that he had a more important appointment to keep. I hadn't known his time was short. Cancer.

The old Finn who had lived for the sky and for the waters, feared an end in an impersonal, white, antiseptic room.

So he chose the time. He chose the place.

When I learned the story, when I comprehended the question, I understood his answer, and I didn't blame him. It made sense. His work was done.

After all, we'd caught the only fish in the whole damn river.
© Tony Bender, 1992

Mama Robin

She flies away, Mama Robin does, every day when we park before the garage doors that hide yet another reorganization so in depth it will not allow indoor parking. Again.

It is a gamble that we will complete, before the first hail, the final unpacking that began well over a year ago when we moved to this country home.

The Redhead battled the barn swallows when we came, those builders of mud nests that clung hideously to the corners of our home. She would knock them down, the birds would rebuild, and the battle would resume.

This year, the swallows have returned, and she beats on the windows at them like Ethel Leesberg did to me when an errant throw would rattle her faded old trailer house like a drum.

But Mama Robin has lodging this spring. It comes at no small price for The Redhead who demands a tidy home—a woman so demanding about appearance that she will not go to the emergency room without a 45 minute session with Mary Kay.

The robin started her nest not much more than seven feet up, on a light fixture between the garage doors. Over the fixture, a remnant of winter battles, we had tossed a 25-foot extension cord that powered Christmas lights and block heaters. Before we believed in winter's end, Mama Robin declared it spring and began building the nest, intertwining the cord with twigs and other construction material.

"Now that ugly old cord will have to hang there half the summer," The Redhead moaned in dismay, when the building began.

We can hear the robin chirp merrily every morning, and Dylan has marked the progress from our excellent living room view. The Redhead boosted him up to see the the pale blue eggs and then I get the report. "The wobin is going to have babies!"

In recent days as endless rains turned our yard into jello, worms slithered to the surface, and the eating has been good for the gaping mouths we now see peeking just above the lip of the nest.

How satisfying it is to drink our morning coffee while Mama Robin serves breakfast outside. She looks a bit thin from all the running around but her posture is proud as The Redhead's when Dylan actually settles in and eats a good meal.

The baby birds are so fat it is hard to imagine they will ever be able to fly. But day by day they grow into their greedy beaks, and one day they will be gone.

Mama Robin will be welcomed back next spring.

But I trust she will have to rebuild.

© Tony Bender, 1999

Big John's Clothes

Things can slide when you're a bachelor. You do dishes when you run out of forks. When the sock drawer is empty, you buy more. You start drinking out of milk cartons. You carry out the trash every February 29. And there's no one to yell at you.

Like I said, things start to slide.

Things started to slide for Big John some time ago.

He didn't expect interference from my mother.

For three Sundays in a row, Mom drove by John's house on her way to church. And every Sunday, she could see the same flannel shirts and trousers dangling from his clothesline. It troubled her. It's something she couldn't help.

There's a gene that women have—The Orderliness Gene—that is multiplied in strength when they become mothers. As a mother of six, Mom has an Orderliness Gene so enlarged it is actually visible to the naked eye.

The Orderliness Gene makes women go to extremes—some actually polish the leaves of their houseplants for cripes' sake. But it's no weirder than the Squalor Gene found in the DNA of men. It fades with marriage but mutates unchecked in the body of a bachelor. Thus you have men who believe a livingroom carpet comprised of Cheetos and cornflakes is a good thing.

Frankly, I'm amazed that my mom could drive by John's laundry even twice without scooping it off the line, sewing on missing buttons and ironing his underwear. She must be getting old.

Anyway, give her credit for holding out for three weeks.

As for John, he claims he was just trying to pack as much of that "fresh air softness" into his dungarees as possible. That's his story anyway. I don't figure it would hold up in court, but us journalists are supposed to tell both sides of the story—even if one is a dang big fib.

But back to our story...

As she drove by John's laundry on the third week, Mom couldn't help herself. She stopped the car and began pulling the clothes off the line.

Technically, you might call it theft, but it's a small town.

Even if the town cop had driven by, the conversation would have gone something like this:

Cop: "Hey, Jan, watcha doin'?"

Mom: "Stealing Big John's laundry."

Cop: "Awwright, jest don't git caught."

Of course, once she had John's clothes there was the quandary of what to do with them. I suppose she could have saved them for the next city rummage sale and let John buy them back, but she decided to box them up and mail them back.

Our local U.S. Postmaster was only too happy to help. He encouraged Mom to send the package postage due. So she did.

She had to wait three days before John got around to getting his mail. Like I said, things start to slide.

As he walked away from the post office, John began opening the box. When he realized what was in it, he did an abrupt U-turn.

"Who sent this?!" he demanded.

But of course, our postal employees are sworn to uphold the

confidentiality of their clients. Collusion is their business.

For weeks, John accused pretty much everyone in town of the chicanery before the truth came out.

My little brother, Mike, the one with the Blabbermouth Gene, spilled the beans. But by then the statute of limitations on clothes heisting had expired.

But trouble may again be brewing.

Just last weekend, Mom mentioned to John that his laundry had been out for an extended period again.

Just a friendly warning.

"They're just rags," he protested. "Don't steal them again!"

Then in that laconic Big John way, he added, "That *was* a good one..."

© Tony Bender, 1997

Coyote Killer

I'll be the first to admit that my method of coyote disposal is not something you'd read about in the NRA handbook. I'm sure if you pick up *Coyote Killer Monthly* or *Guns and Ammo*, you're not going to find pictures of a guy stomping barefoot through the snow in a bathrobe. But that's how I did it.

We've long suspected it was coyotes who did in our beloved Brittany, Duck Dog, and our golden retriever pup, Buddy, but we never expected to see a coyote insolently chewing a deer carcass right in our back yard at 8 a.m.

Normally that wouldn't happen, but our pony-sized German short hair, Little Man, had abandoned his post for his weekly visit to our neighbor, LeMar Haas. LeMar says Little Man has been a big help during calving season. Not one killer grouse has gotten close to a newborn calf.

I was stretching, trying to coax some circulation into my bones, when I spotted the coyote. At first I thought it was the neighbors' dog but he wasn't that big. The Mehrers have a hound that fetches old threshing machines to stay in hunting trim. Still, this was a large coyote—on his way to becoming a wolf.

I was hoping to find my Grandpa's old 30-30 in the closet, but all of my guns had been moved to a storage space when we laid carpet in the bedroom. They were all cased and hopelessly out of order, so I opened the case on the top. A 12 gauge pump.

I didn't expect to get close enough to do much harm with a scatter gun, but I didn't figure I had much more time.

I slapped a couple shells in as I tiptoed out the front door. The wind was against me so he didn't smell me. At 60 feet, I let him have it as The Redhead and Dylan watched from the bedroom. I was really hoping he would stay down. Because—even though I've never experienced it—I'm sure having a possibly rabid, ticked off coyote gnawing on your bare legs, is not the optimum way to start the morning.

The surprising part of the whole incident is how it raised my standing in the household. Heretofore, I was known as the guy who couldn't operate a screwdriver. The Anti-Bob Vila. In one blast of my trusty Remington, I became a modern day Davy Crockett. I even started to talk a little like John Wayne. Said howdy instead of hello. Started calling everyone Pilgrim.

Dylan told everyone at day care about Daddy, the Coyote Killer, and I overheard The Redhead talking to her parents on the phone, "I always wondered why he had all those guns...He can actually shoot!"

I tried to be cool about the whole deal, but as Allan Burke, the editor of the Linton paper said, "How many editors do you suppose shot a coyote in a bathrobe this week?"

"Actually," I corrected, "*I* was wearing the bathrobe."

Still, Allen thought it was a fairly big deal.

So I felt okay about bragging a bit.

When big city telemarketers called, I filled them in.

Salesman: "How are you today Mr. Bender."

Me: "I killed a coyote this morning."

Salesman: "Uhh, yeah... Say, we have a new line of colors in our paper stock..."

Me: "That reminds me, I was wearing a hunter green

bathrobe when I slayed the beast. Got any hunter green?"

Salesman: "Actually, Mr. Bender, these are pastels..."

Me: "Hey, you ever shoot a coyote?"

CLICK.

I have to admit I milked it.

When The Redhead would start to chide me for leaving my dirty socks on the floor, I puffed up my chest and replied, "Yep, I shot a coyote..."

She'd crumble, feel my biceps and get me a beer.

The coyote killing had The Redhead looking at me in a new light. Let's face it, chicks dig a little testosterone display. Sure, they'll tell you not to get into a bar fight, but I'll bet if you just haul off and pop that annoying drunk the next time, she'll be impressed.

If you could beat up an obnoxious coyote in a bar, while wearing a green bathrobe, it would even be better.

© Tony Bender, 1999

Come home, he said.

"Come home," he said and I knew he was right. It had been six months at least.

The visit was always next week or next time. I was too tired or had too much work to do.

But it wasn't like him to call. In all the years I've known him I only remember him calling me once before. So I listened.

"Come home," he said. "Come home and see my dad," he said. "Come home and see your dad."

A few weeks before I had called his father in that hospital room a prairie away. I called instead of employing florists, I kidded, because I was sure flowers would have offended his manhood.

So we talked about the weather, of hunting pheasants—of simple things. I told him to hang in there. I had no magic words to say. But it wasn't the substance of the call that mattered, it was that the call was made.

That meant a lot to him, his son told me, but now it was time to do more. So I packed my bags.

His father was always bigger than life. He blustered and snorted. He could be loud and ornery—and that's what we all loved about him. He was our John Wayne.

While his son was my best friend and our sisters were the same, our fathers held brawls in the streets. Fistfights.

But showing wisdom that adults rarely do, the children kept their friendship strong. We were welcomed in each other's homes. Silly fathers be damned. Eventually, they too came around. Harold would bring my father fresh vegetables in season and fish when the catch was good. And when Harold was sick, my father cheered him on.

I don't know—and I suppose I never will—how or why they managed to mend fences. But I know what they accomplished. They completed the bond between two families.

I wanted to get one more crazy haircut before I visited. It was a ritual. I would appear with my hair dyed, braided, permed or spiked, and Harold would unkindly critique each one—to my delight.

Even when I was in Alaska, at the other end of the continent, I would get a strange trim and think, "Harold would really hate this." When I visited with an earring dangling from one ear, he remarked, "Yuh damn pirate!"

When I got there, we visited for a while—Harold and me —about snow, pheasants... things like that. I almost felt like apologizing for my hair. But it wasn't the conversation that was important...

"Goodby, Harold," I said when it was time to go. "I don't know when I'll see you again..." Then I let go of his hand and bit my lip. And he bit his because we both knew I was saying more.

"Have you told your father that you love him?" my friend asked. We were cruising nighttime gravel roads at 10 mph. Therapy by the mile.

The question took me by surprise and I had to think. "Not lately," I said. "Not enough."

How do you tell a giant of a man that you love him, the

big man's son wondered. He must know... maybe it isn't necessary...

"Just tell him," I counseled hypocritically. "But say it or you'll regret it forever. Tell him."

I got the news from an answering machine. Sometimes I really hate that blinking green light. I tried to call, but at times like that phones are busy. So I sat down and tried to write.

When he called me, I just didn't want to hear him say it. Before he could say more than my name, I cut him off: "I know, Gary. Mom called."

Then I had to ask... "Did you get to talk to him?"

"Yes, I told him that I loved him," he said and then added in an I-told-you-so-manner, "He knew."

"I'm glad. I'm glad you got to tell him," I said lamely.

This time I sent flowers from my family to his, and I hoped the giant would understand. Then I headed back for one more goodbye. Because there wasn't time for a haircut, I came with it slicked back. Harold would have hated it.

© Tony Bender, 1992

Sons Lost

I was nearly ready for bed when he appeared at the door. Best friends can do that even when you haven't spoken in months.

He was still gritty from work in the fields, his face black. He had driven an hour to get here.

"I just needed to talk," he said.

I offered him a beer. He refused, but I would have one. We'd shared many over the years on those late night cruises down gravel trails, sometimes going hours without speaking.

It was a our ritual.

He speaks seldom of the demons who sometimes perch on all of our shoulders; those who would corner us, forcing us to claw bloodily back or cower in sorrow. But now he needed to talk. True to form, he did not say much. But I filled in the silences with consolations tender, and perspectives harsh. His mother was gravely ill and now, it seemed, he would lose his son.

In six months, the bond between father and son had become like steel but around them, their lives were careening precariously beyond their control, at break-neck speed, kamikaze pilots at the wheel.

Such beautiful children cannot be accidents, but this boy was born even as relationships around him crumbled.

They had tried. But she was moving out, and my friend

would lose his son.

The next day, I demanded a dinner invitation from my mother. As we rolled into town from the west, my son and wife and I, we spotted my friend on the lonely Main Street.

He was holding the child.

I rolled down my window, and the boy beamed at me, bright eyes grinning in concert with a toothless smile.

We made small talk as we admired the boy. His father told me there would be no reconciliation. And now he would have to walk the half block and give the child up, he told me with halting tones and desperate eyes.

He turned abruptly to hide the tears, and I turned to do the same.

There was nothing I could do.

Days later, I heard my wife wail as she paged through the newspaper I had purchased days before. He was 22, the obituary read, the only son of a friend. Julie hadn't seen the boy since he was 10 or 12, a handsome tow-headed boy. At 22, he ended his splendid existence. She mourned. She regretted not knowing, not being there.

Then, later that day, darkness got darker when she got the call at work. Another friend had lost a brother. Another suicide. Some damnable epidemic. Nineteen. Nineteen is newborn. Nineteen is spring. A flash of lightning. Nineteen is too damn young.

She would make this funeral, to stand defiant even as young men were buried, to confront the demons. For she has a son. And they must know they cannot have him.

The sister called that night, and Julie spoke in soothing tones to comfort her. "Is there anything I can do?" she asked. "Just ask, and it will be done."

There was a pause at the other end. Well, the sister confided, she was concerned there would be no flowers. "Could you please send some flowers?"

After the funeral, Julie shared her day with me as I read the brief obituary. She hadn't known the boy and he was a stranger to me, too. So I was surprised by my grief. And my anger. "Stupid kid," I cursed as I threw down the church bulletin.

It turned out there were lots of flowers.

© Tony Bender, 2000

Stop. Rewind.

*S*top. Rewind.

Glass leaps from the pavement and heals itself.

Fenders uncrumple.

Air bags deflate and return to their hiding place in the dash.

Bones unbreak.

Blood unbleeds.

The nightmare reverses.

Oh, how Jason Doe would love to rewind that whole night. Get back to the pool table. Flirt again with the girl he was supposed to meet later.

And in the replay, he doesn't get behind the wheel. And he never meets Cari Bailey. She's 20, lively and pretty. They go through their lives, passing in Bismarck checkout counters, on sidewalks, never meeting.

And it's a blessing.

Stop. Rewind.

The ball bounces high off the rim and amidst taller players, a 5-10 gazelle sweeps the ball from the rim. The fast break is cut off, so he pulls up at the three point line. The net sings sweetly and Hettinger has three more.

He's quiet, this kid. A bit of a gym rat. Got a shy smile. Gentle. Decent. The kind of kid you'd be proud to call your son.

More than once I go home and tell my wife, "We should adopt him." And I half mean it. But Jason has a family. Good folks. Nice people. They raise their kids right.

My heart sinks when I read the story of Cari Bailey's senseless death. Her car is struck broadside by a speeding Pontiac. Jason's name leaps from the print. I pray there is another Jason Doe. Just like Cari's family prays there is some mistake when they get the news.

Neither prayer is answered.

The Cari Bailey I read about is a kind, sweet, pretty, lively girl. A girl with plans for her life. A good kid.

The Jason Doe I read about is a stranger. This 23-year-old is charged with manslaughter. A letter to the editor rants about the usual lawyerly posturing over bail. Jason's roommate grants a damning interview. "I don't know what he was thinking," he says. This isn't the Jason Doe I know.

Stop. Rewind.

At the state track meet Jason lands in the sand pit after soaring farther than anyone. He brings home a first place medal. But he's not the type to brag. Just hard-working and determined.

The Jason I read about in successive front page stories is demonized. This tragedy has a princess, and Jason certainly cannot be the prince, so he becomes the dragon.

But I know enough about Jason Doe to know he would trade his life for Cari Bailey's in a heartbeat.

It would be so much easier if he did not have a conscience. If he had spent his life as some unfeeling, lawless creature, we could slap him behind bars with satisfaction.

There can be no satisfaction here. There can be no tidy ending.

No ringing moral tale.

Just the sad lesson that the innocent can be swept away in a moment from their families. A cold slap of a reminder that some mistakes can cost us very dearly.

One beautiful child has killed another.

And that tape, that damn tape, won't rewind.

© Tony Bender, 1999

Writer's note: Jason Doe was sentenced to serve time at the North Dakota State Penitentiary.

He Fixed Things

Every town has one. One old man to fix the broken toys. One old man to tell the stories. One old man to bring us joy.

In Ashley, ND, where I was born, it was Mr. Miller. He made wooden moons with petite shelves for knick-knacks to hang on Mom's walls . His garage was loaded with them. They were scattered among the sawdust, and each one was unique. He made glorious birdhouses, and I remember erecting his creations in the yards of my youth. A pale green home for sparrows stood proudly in our yard, and a huge red birdhouse survives to this very day. It could house overweight ostriches.

In Frederick, SD, where I grew up, the place I call my hometown, there was another man. Cut from the same cloth. Same Union. God or Fate or Luck deposited my family next door. We rented his house while he lived in the faded green trailer to the west. Somehow it didn't seem fair that Glenn and Ethel should live in a closet while we lived in a castle.

It seemed that way to me then. There were wooden pillars that separated the living and dining rooms, fancy hanging light fixtures and two bathrooms. The house had two porches, and the front screens soon became bowed from the force of whiffle balls missed by inept batsmen. This, of course, didn't please Ethel, but Glenn never said a word and once in awhile he replaced the screens. And then we had a fresh backstop.

Glenn would fix our bikes and assemble new toys. His stored paint in our basement became community property, and my two-wheeler soon was a horrid maroon.

He'd drag home wrecked cars to dismantle, though he never found the time. Seems he could never let anything go to waste. That old Ford soon became a permanent third base.

When Glenn was finally retired from his job at the Ford Garage, it hurt us almost as much as it hurt him. He still had a lot of years left to give. We knew that. He knew that. They got lost in the numbers. But it all turned out for the best. He had more time to fix our dented screens and our wobbly bikes, and he had more time to go fishing. He loved to fish. We ate the extras, and his mangy cats got the rest.

Fishing wasn't enough to keep him occupied, and soon every odd job that needed doing was being done by Glenn. He could do anything...or at least he thought he could and most everyone believed him.

I remember Glenn and "Shorty" coming over to fix an electrical malady that had plagued the family. In classic Abbott and Costello style, they argued over who would have to torture aged knees to test the socket near the floor. Glenn finally decreed that it should be Shorty since he was built closer to the floor. I don't remember if they ever solved the problem or what the final charge was, but in entertainment value it was a bargain.

After Ethel had passed on, Mom and Dad would invite Glenn over for supper, and he'd tell the same old stories over again. A wicked mimic, Mom would go, "To make a short story reallllly long..." in perfect imitation of Glenn. But it was done in fun, and we loved hearing those old stories as much as he loved telling them.

It was Mom who called to tell me that Glenn had died. She

never calls unless it's really important. I hate it when she calls.

At the funeral I sat beside little brother, Mike. He cried as we sat in the pew nearest the coffin. I wanted to comfort him, but I didn't know how. I was crying, too.

Now, at the Community Store, where everyone meets for 8 a.m. coffee, one chair is still vacant. No one dares sit there. It's Glenn's chair.

© Tony Bender, 1992

The Boycott

I don't know if this thing between my relatives and South Dakota is going to develop into a full-fledged shooting war or not, but it's clearly become a pretty good feud.

See, my step-dad, Jim, is boycotting the City of Aberdeen over a water bill dispute. And my Uncle Doug is boycotting the whole state over a speeding ticket.

Jim, who lives with my mom in Frederick, SD, 25 miles north of Aberdeen, is pretty steamed over the whole thing. What happened was, he rented out his house in Aberdeen to a deadbeat who refused to pay the rent. Of course, eviction proceedings take months, and by the time he got the guy out of there, the place was trashed. So not only was he out a lot of rent money, he was stuck with the cost of repairs. On top of that, the City of Aberdeen came after him for his renter's water bill. According to the law, the property owner is responsible. Well, laws are laws and right is right. Jim took his cause to court where the judge sided with the city. "I'll never spend another dime in Aberdeen," Jim vowed in the courtroom.

Then there's Uncle Doug who got picked up in a tricky 45 mile an hour speed zone going 65 miles an hour. Bam. $100 fine.

This upset Doug so much he wrote a nasty letter to the editor. He even penned a note to South Dakota Governor Bill Janklow, complaining about the rednecks in Aberdeen.

Janklow, who apparently failed diplomacy class in charm school, responded with a letter of his own. To paraphrase, it pretty much said, "Tough noogies."

This made Doug so mad he won't even spit in South Dakota.

Jim, meanwhile, has been dragging my mother 75 miles north to Jamestown, ND, to do their shopping. I don't know if it's important to the story or not, but I suppose at this point I should note that Jim is Polish.

Over Thanksgiving dinner, I leaned over to Jim, "So has (Mayor) Tim Rich surrendered yet?"

Of course, he hadn't. So I suggested we drive to Aberdeen to throw eggs at the mayor's house. We had to scrub the mission when we realized we'd have to drive to Jamestown to get eggs.

So instead I called Mayor Rich.

"Your highness," I said, "Are you aware my family is boycotting Aberdeen?"

"As a matter of fact," he whispered, "Just between you and me, we had a top secret meeting over the loss of revenue from the Frederick contingent just this morning." He sounded worried.

I also informed him that my uncle was slandering the name of Aberdeen all over the place and refused to venture across the border. Mayor Rich was familiar with Doug's letter. Pretty tough stuff, he agreed.

"On top of all that," I railed, "there's the further humiliation of the letter from Governor Janklow."

Mayor Rich noted that he thought there had been a decrease in traffic from the north. "This could cost us federal highway funds," he allowed.

This is a man whose administration is facing a serious crisis. I figured Jim and Doug had him on the ropes so I asked, "Well, are you ready to surrender or not?"

"Well, I'd surrender unconditionally this minute if it were up to me," he confessed. "But since my Commander in Chief doesn't appear willing to give up, that would be insubordination. I'd be exiled to Jamestown." I said I understood.

"We're really sorry about all this," he said. "We don't want anyone to be mad at us." He sounded sincere. "Whatever, you do, please don't make me come off like some arrogant jerk," he pleaded. I promised to do what I could. He really was very nice.

Then I hopped on the other line to call Pierre. I got the governor's secretary. I informed her that my family was boycotting South Dakota—which seemed to upset her a great deal.

"You're kidding!"

"Nope, and I'm wondering if you're seeing a connection between that and the drop in tourism this year."

I think that irritated her.

"Anyway, I just wanted to talk to the governor to see if he was ready to surrender."

But the governor was out. I'm guessing he'll get back to me about the time they finish the Crazy Horse Monument.

I was really hoping we could get this thing worked out. Every time I'm home and Mom sends me out for a loaf of bread, it's like a three hour round trip.

© Tony Bender, 1997

Writer's note: Mayor Rich lost his next election. When I heard the news, I called my mother. "Is Jim dancing in the street," I asked.

"Naked," she replied.

Horse Pee

There was a time when I felt comfortable insulting a heifer on the run. I'd honk my horn and yell, "stupid cow!" Or if I was walking in the pasture and stepped where I shouldn't have, I'd cuss. "Dang cow pie."

But those days could be coming to an end if the North Dakota Legislature passes the Animal Excrement Sedition Act, House Bill 1176.

What the bill says is, you could get your butt sued off if you say uncomplimentary things about agricultural products.

Like, for instance, if I were to call the bill's sponsors *pea brains*, that could be interpreted as uncomplimentary toward peas. Boom. Lawsuit.

However, if you refer to these lawmakers as dimwits, you'll be OK because a dimwit is not an agricultural product.

If you complain to the waiter that your steak is a little gristly, chances are you'll do hard time in the big house. And heaven help you if you even think the words *Mad Cow Disease.* Expect a perfunctory execution.

This could really affect some time-tested cliches. If you say, "You can't get blood from a turnip," the entire turnip industry could turn on you like a mad dog. (Ohh oh, now I've insulted mad dogs which could lead to a lawsuit by the Mad Dog Breeders of America.)

This whole thing started because PETA, the People for the

Ethical Treatment of Animals, began saying derogatory things about the 29 horse urine producers in the state.

Before this, I thought PETA was some sort of bread but apparently they are horse urine insulters of the worst kind.

This has caused no small problem on the urine farms. Their livelihood has been insulted, and if you can't be proud of being a urine farmer, then dagnabbit, there's something terribly wrong.

This whole controversy has enlightened me. There was a time when I might sample a poor wine and describe it as *tasting like horse urine*— although not in those words exactly. No more. I have seen the error of my politically incorrect ways. Heck, I even had bumper stickers made up: *Honk if you love horse pee!*

My mother asked me about the bumper sticker, which caused quite a stir last weekend when I drove her to church. When I explained that it might soon be illegal to say bad things about overripe melons, Mom got concerned. She's an old-time melon thumper from way back.

"But what about the First Amendment? What about free speech?" she asked.

"Don't you think the First Amendment pales in significance when it comes to the hurt feelings of those poor urine farmers?" I countered. "I sure wouldn't want someone making snide remarks about my urine. Besides, similar legislation has already passed in 12 other states..."

"If 12 states jumped off a bridge, would you?"

One of the states that has passed an Ag-Insult Bill is Idaho. After giving it some thought, I realized that could lead to some problems if North Dakota passes the bill. Idaho claims to grow the best potatoes. To my mind that suggests that maybe North

Dakota potatoes are inferior. Heck, we'd be honor bound to sue.

So reluctantly, I have to withdraw my support for this bill. As much as I admire horse urine farmers, I fear that this bill may actually require the medical community to endorse E coli infested chicken as a healthy source of fatal disease.

Zoning commissions may have to censure anyone who suggests that a large swine operation is odoriferous.

Juvenile crime will skyrocket. Some day your child is going to be in the lunch line innocently proclaiming that he doesn't like green beans. Imagine the nasty publicity when you're dragged into court for defamation of the Jolly Green Giant.

Ultimately, I think we have to have faith in the free market system. Good products will always be successful. You just have to believe that the general public is going to see through the scurrilous attacks on horse urine. Americans know a good thing when they see it.

© Tony Bender, 1997

Writer's note: The bill passed.

Dear Dave Barry

"*North Dakota, because of poor participation with the 1990 census, wound up reporting that it had a total of only seven residents (the actual number is believed to be much closer to nine). As a result, today North Dakota has zero representatives in Congress and may no longer even be part of the United States. (Somebody should go up there and check.)*"
—**Dave Barry, Miami Herald, March 30, 2000**

Dear Dave,

I just wanted you to know—so you wouldn't lie awake nights wondering—North Dakota is still here.

Your comments about our admittedly sparse population got me concerned, so I checked with my local Census Bureau Head Counter, Byron Drucker in Danzig, "Garden Spot of McIntosh County."

Byron informed me that your figures are way off. He's already at "'lebben" and says the count could go as high as "twenny" if it gets warm enough for him to remove his shoes.

As to your assertion that North Dakota may not even have congressional representation, I asked around and local Republicans assured me you are absolutely correct.

However, after further intense research, I discovered North Dakota, the World Leader in Fine Liver Sausage, does indeed have at least one congressman, Sen. Byron Dorgan, D-ND. (North Dakota also leads the nation in Byrons.)

One of the reasons North Dakota has so few politicians is when they are done creating new legislation (mostly about cows), they leave the state.

Former governors George Sinner and Allen Olson have moved to Minnesota, where ironically, they have embarked on new careers as professional wrestlers.

The two ex-governors returned last year, joining other former governors, to offer North Dakotans advice about fixing all the things their administrations screwed up.

Generally, the advice consisted of "grabbing opportunity in a sleeper hold" and "beating back adversity with a folding chair."

Sadly, this trend of politicians leaving our state started with **Teddy Roosevelt**, the 26th president, who before leaving for Washington, D.C., ranched in the Badlands near Medora, confusing cowpokes and cows alike with orders such as "Hasten forward quickly there!" (Git along, little doggie.)

Other famous North Dakotans who have left our state include **Bobby Vee** (whose real name is Byron). I'm sure you remember Bobby's famous Sixties protest anthems, *Rubber Ball* and *Take Good Care of My Baby.* (Incidentally—and I'll bet you didn't know this—Bob Dylan once played keyboards in Bobby's band. That was early in Dylan's career before he figured out that a harmonica was a lot easier to lug to gigs than a Steinway.)

Another favorite son of North Dakota is Strasburg musician **Lawrence Welk,** who, along with the movie *Fargo,* helped introduce the "Nor' Duhkoduh" accent to the rest of America. Around here, we really do say, "wunnerful, wunnerful" but rarely in reference to the weather in January.

When we feed livestock, we "trow da cow over da fence some hay." And when we come home, we always "park da car in da crotch (garage)."

Lawrence Welk was famous for his champagne music, but I doubt you could find one bottle of the bubbly in Strasburg. I will guarantee you can find "Redeye," a popular drink made from Everclear and possibly, jet fuel.

Peggy Lee, the sultry singer of *Fever*, is from Jamestown, ND. Her records are still very popular with Rex Reed.

Jamestown is also the home of the World's Largest Concrete Buffalo which measures 26 feet at the hump (or in centimeters, forty milliondy-kabillion).

North Dakotans are real big on massive animal statues. If you ever visit, you'll want to see **New Salem Sue**, the world's largest Holstein cow. You haven't lived until you've joined the citizens of New Salem for the annual Breakfast Under the Udder.

Another large animal structure recently was erected at Steele, ND—a crane. There was a huge debate about naming the crane with "Sandy" narrowly edging out "Dr. Frasier."

Though there are more famous North Dakotans I would love to tell you about—Phil Jackson, Angie Dickinson, Warren Christopher, Roger Maris, Louis L'Amour and Eric Severeid—the aspect of North Dakota of which I am most proud, is the fact that we lead the nation in production of pregnant mare urine.

We had a big stink about the whole thing a while back when PETA, which I believe stands for People Eating Tasty Animals, got upset about urine farmers relentlessly forcing their horses to urinate.

As I understand it, this is accomplished by making the horses to drink vast quantities of beer. (If you ever wondered what those Clydesdales have to do with beer, this might be a clue.)

Curiously, the mares often refuse to urinate, except in groups of three or more. With all this criticism of North Dakota's urine farmers going on, our legislature made it illegal for anyone to criticize North Dakota horse urine, which I would like to point out, is delightfully delicate, yet sassy and slightly pungent in consistency.

Well Dave, that's my report. If you don't believe me, I welcome you to be my guest at Wishek's 75th Annual Sauerkraut Day in mid-October for free wieners and kraut. I'll even set you up with some Redeye.

Sincerely,
Tony Bender

© Tony Bender, 2000

Barry responded: "Dear Tony, Thanks for confirming the existence of <u>South</u> Dakota and inviting me to Sauerkraut Day, which unfortunately I cannot attend because I have... um... some excuse. But really, thanks.—Dave Barry."

The Campaign

DANZIG, ND—Everyone here at Bender For Governor Campaign Headquarters is still pretty shook up. You probably heard about it on the news, but a guy can't believe anything he hears nowadays, and only half of what he sees.

That's why I'm here to give you a first-person account of what happened. First, let me assure you I am all right; I didn't get a scratch.

I was giving my patented rebel-rouser campaign speech here at a fund raiser—you know, the one about a ring of liver sausage in every kettle, etc.

I was just getting to the part about annexing Saskatchewan when this nutball jumps on my egg crate and tries to clonk me with a can of kippered snacks.

He was shouting something like "Viva la pickled herring," and let me tell you, I thought I was a goner for sure. That's when Homer S. Oddsee, using a move he learned on prom night to escape the clutches of Betty Jolene Snerdsack, subdued the rascal.

I am a grateful man. "Homer," I says, "Thanks. Getting killed by kippered snacks is about the last thing I want carved into my tombstone."

"Aww, they wouldn't have killed you," said the ever-modest Homer. "Not unless you ate 'em."

The kippered snack assassin turned out to be a local Norwegian, which explains a lot of things. The cops say he was hopped up on lutefisk.

Now, I'm no prohibitionist, but I have grave concerns about the over-the-counter sale of lutefisk and kippered snacks.

Registration of lutefisk with stiff penalties for violators is a must. But I am against outlawing preserved fish products altogether. When kippered snacks are outlawed, only Norwegians will have kippered snacks.

I have challenged my competitors, Heidi Heitkamp and John Hoeven, to take a similar stand.

I had a conversation the other day with Heidi, but we didn't discuss lutefisk regulation.

I was at Minot for the debate between Heitkamp and Hoeven when I ran into her. I was fairly upset about not being invited to take part in the debate, but then it was explained that the winner of the Heitkamp/Hoeven debates will move up to challenge me. It's sort of based on the NFL wild-card playoff system, as I understand it.

After all my snotty little comments about North Dakota politicians in this column, I was a little nervous when Heidi sat down at my table.

That's the trouble with North Dakota. If you write something about someone, you will eventually have to look them in the eye. Why just the other day, I received a note from U.S. Sen. Byron Dorgan who read a recent column I wrote documenting the fact that 67 percent of North Dakotans, including, tragically, some women, are named Byron.

The good senato wrote that when he was born in Regent, ND, his parents had considered naming him Tony. But they looked in the phone book and there were something like 46

111

Tonys in there.

But I stray. My point is, a guy can't write anything in North Dakota without being called to account for it. That is why my published exaggerations are completely factual except for the parts that aren't.

Anyway, as I recall, my conversation with Heidi went something like this:

"You're Tony Bender, aren't you?

"Uhh, no," I replied, sweating bullets. "Jack Zaleski, *Fargo Forum*."

"My God, Jack, What happened to you!?"

"Car accident," I said.

Wouldn't you know those officers picked that moment to serve the summons, and my cover was blown.

"I've been reading your columns," Heidi said.

I disavowed any knowledge of my actions.

"I'm upset about it too, Heidi," I said. I can't believe someone would distribute that kind of outrageous stuff using my good name!"

"Some of it is just hilarious."

"Well, the funny stuff is mine," I allowed.

"So how is your campaign going?" she wondered.

I puffed up my chest. "Got $12.50 in the old war chest," I told her. "I've been spending it on beer. Do you think that's wrong?"

I must say she is a good sport. (Here comes part of the column that is mostly true.) She reached into her purse and gave me a buck.

Wow. John Hoeven certainly hadn't contributed to my campaign, I told her.

And you know what? She pulled out another dollar for

John. I was impressed. You hear about these political races turning into bare-knuckle affairs. I decided right then to only write really nasty stuff about folks who don't give me dollars for my campaign.

Wouldn't you know Heidi turned up in Wishek a few days later, and we had one of those George W. Bush/John McCain summits, except Heidi is a Democrat and I'm an agnostic.

"Heidi," I said, "I've been giving serious thought to your campaign platform and I am convinced that at the very least, you would make a fine lt. governor."

© Tony Bender, 2000

Writer's note: John Hoeven, who resigned his post as head of the Bank of North Dakota to run for governor, sent me a dollar in the mail after this column was published. I wrote him back, thanking him for the donation. Noting the dollar was well-worn, I guessed it must have been in his pocket a long while. "You must be a very good banker," I wrote.

Campaign Goes Awry

I don't want to alarm the nine voters who have pledged their support to the *Bender for Governor Campaign,* but our strategy of scrawling free advertising on bathroom stalls across the state has yet to make a real impact other than to force us to spend valuable campaign resources bailing out our people.

My attorney, Tom Secrest, contends that there is a huge difference between vandalism and our campaign poetry:

To the voter on the can,
Tony Bender is the man,
Number one or a pooper,
He is great and he is super,
A Bender vote makes us happy,
Otherwise, we'll all feel crappy.

We had folks writing this little ditty in every outhouse and rest stop on I-94, along with: *For a good time call Tony at 1-555-KUCHENS.*

Secrest is fighting these arrests on two fronts. First, he says, our freedom of speech has been abridged. Besides, he told the judge, "We're just keeping campaign advertising where it belongs!" Despite the impassioned defense, the case was harmed irreparably when the defendant, Gottlieb Snerdley, kept pointing at the judge and asking loudly, "Who's the Druid?"

That, and the fact that it's an election year for the judge, whose campaign slogan is, *I'll convict everyone but you,* causes me great concern.

Back at campaign headquarters, these setbacks have everyone pretty nervous. My campaign strategist, Otto Szenrkg, (It sounds just like it's spelled.), working out of our Zeeland office on the third stool from the door, tells me we have to modify our game plan.

So far our campaign has focused on liver sausage feeds and buying rounds at the local bars. While it would clearly be foolish to abandon this enlightened strategy, we decided to take a page from candidates across the state.

First, we have to comment on any major news event. It's important to have a learned opinion on absolutely everything. And we must automatically disagree with the other candidates' opinions, even when they make sense. (Admittedly, a rare scenario.)

After I saw the headline, *School Bus Runs Down Goat Herd*, in a major daily paper, I knew I had a golden opportunity, so I called the editor.

"I want to take a stand on education," I said.

"What's that?" he responded eagerly.

"I am firmly against goats getting run over by school buses..."

"Uhh..."

"Furthermore, it is obvious by this indiscriminate goat violence, that the present administration has lost control..."

At that point, by a nasty turn of fate, I was disconnected.

I fully expected to see a big news story in the next morning's paper. There was. *Editor Granted Restraining Order Against Goat Advocate*, the headline read.

Now, I don't want to disparage big city editors, but it is obvious that many are descendant from a long line of goat killers.

After that, we decided to focus our efforts on small town newspaper editors because they actually feel honor bound to let a candidate speak.

We come in and throw around platitudes about how we're for higher grain prices, lower gas prices, higher teacher salaries, lower taxes and higher wages for the working man—as long as local businessmen don't have to pay them.

Then we pose for photographs looking confident but concerned. Typically, after the struggling, well-meaning weekly newspaper publishes our free publicity, we will purchase television ads because the largest voter bloc to whom we hope to appeal is borderline illiterate. And because TV stations need our money to continue broadcasting socially relevant fare such as *Big Brother* and *The Young and the Restless.*

My commercial is pretty much the norm. It opens, panning across waves of golden grain under a sunny, blue sky. Then I walk into the scene, wearing a flannel shirt, top button undone, sleeves rolled up like I just set down my pitchfork.

I am looking confident but concerned about your problems.

The camera pulls back to reveal my perfect family. The Redhead is gorgeous in a windblown sort of way, and she looks at me adoringly, as I maintain a bold but approachable stance, with a confident yet concerned expression.

Four-year old Dylan looks precocious but well-mannered in a fidgety sort of way. He is not even picking his nose.

The music swells majestically and a dignified, authoritative voice intones, "Vote for Bender. He's swell."

Hard-hitting. To the point.

I think we're gonna win this thing.

© Tony Bender, 2000

Editor's note: After writing this column, Dick Pence, who wrote a great dog story in his book Two Longs and a Short, e-mailed advising me to use a dog in the commercial.

I responded:

After considerable thought, I decided to abide by your advice and include a dog in my commercial. The edited version of my column is hereby presented to you for your consideration:

The camera pulls back to reveal my perfect family. The Redhead is gorgeous in a windblown sort of way, and she looks at me adoringly, as I maintain a bold but approachable stance, with a confident yet concerned expression. Four-year old Dylan looks precocious but well-mannered in a fidgety sort of way. He is not even picking his nose. The family dog, a flop-eared springer spaniel, is briskly humping my left knee. He looks confident but concerned. The music swells majestically and a dignified, authoritative voice intones, "Vote for Bender. He's swell."

Then Dick wrote back:

"Good. Excellent, in fact. You are too young to remember, but in 1962, McGovern made his second run for the U.S. Senate. He had lost in 1960 to Karl Mundt and this time he started out running against Francis Case. But Case died and the South Dakota Republican governor appointed a power company attorney by the name of Joe Bottum to Case's seat. Bottum was well on his way to victory but the GOP decided to nail things down by buying a half hour's worth of prime time on all the TV stations in the state. Which at that time was one —Sioux Falls and its towers at Garden City and Reliance. Since video tape hadn't been invented yet and recording equipment (kinescope) of the day was too expensive for a tiny SD station, the program was broadcast live across the state.

Joe Bottum sat in his living room, concerned but confident, discussing the issues of the day. Like what a disaster it would be if SD actually elected a Democrat. The half hour was drawing to a close and the camera pulled back to a wide shot. There was the Bottum family in front of the fire place, Joe in his easy chair, his faithful dog by his side, his wife standing, concerned but confident, behind him near the mantle of the fire place, the children—one boy and one girl—smiling from their spot on the floor nearby. As the camera took all this in, Joe made his final point, glanced back at his wife and asked, "Isn't that right, dear?"

Mrs. Bottum, who apparently hadn't seen the script, replied: "Isn't what right?" Hastily the camera went to a tighter shot of Joe in his chair with his faithful dog by his side. Joe, concerned but confident, smiled at the people of South Dakota and leaned over to pet his dog. The dog bit his hand just as the camera was fading out.

After about three recounts, McGovern was declared the winner by about a dozen votes. Be careful of the damned dog."

—Dick Pence

No More Nickels

Grandma made dandelion wine. I was no more than seven when I first tasted it. And I have searched in the years since to recapture that bitter-sweet taste.

I was immortal then and so was Grandma. She could always make more, I might have thought—if my unformed jellied brain had not been enthralled with living.

Much of what Grandma was came from her mother. I knew her as Grandma Joachim. I would visit my great-grandmother almost daily when the school day was done.

She made "Russian Tea" from a plant that grew around the tiny trailer house that was her home. She made cookies for me while I paged through picture books filled with somber faces I would never know. Yet their blood runs through my veins.

The highlight of the visit was the nickel that she would pull from her coin purse.

I was a mercenary visitor.

When Grandma Joachim died, it was her daughter who took my hand and led me to the casket. As Grandma Bender and I looked down at the shell of what had been, she squeezed my hand. "No more nickels," she said.

My memories of Grandma Bender are much more vivid. We had more time together. I spent summers there and would have grown fat on the rich German delicacies had Grandpa and Grandma not seen to it that I develop my skills as a bale hauler.

Nobody worked harder than Grandma.

One day, out in the field, we came upon a very young rabbit—it's mother was dead. Grandma picked it up, and when I realized she meant to dispatch it, I pleaded for its life. I lost the case and the bunny lost its life. She thought it better to end its life with a quick twist of the neck than have it starve or become a meal for a fox.

But Grandma was far from heartless. If you were quick, you could catch her eyes smiling. She could spot a drinker a mile away, and when Grandpa walked in the door after a social visit at George's Bar, she would chew him out for having "chicken eyes." She ended every argument with Grandpa with a simple statement: "Ach Benny, you're so dumb."

Theirs was not a romantic partnership. Grandpa tells me that when he asked her to marry him, all she did was shrug her shoulders as if to say, "Well, I'm not doing anything else for the rest of my life." With a simple shrug of the shoulders, my father came into existence as did I some years later.

At Christmas, she would get modern kitchen conveniences from her thoughtful children and grandchildren. But at the end of the day the new mixers and toaster ovens would be stowed in the attic with last year's loot. She was "saving it for nice," she told us. We still quote her today.

Today when any Bender gets a gift you can see a glint come to his eye and a grin to his face. "I'm gonna save it for nice," is the punch line that always gets a laugh.

A beautiful crocheted doily lies on my old oak table. Grandma made one for all of us grandkids. I've had it for years, but only lately could I bring myself to put it on display. I guess I was saving it for nice.

Grandma left us dozens of crocheted masterpieces. And for

two years after her death we dined on her famous kuchen and homemade noodles. The freezer was one of the only modern appliances she ever used.

Her whole life was a service to those she loved and when a stroke took the use of her hands she felt useless.

"I wish I could die," she told me. "Well, Grandma, I can't say I would wish otherwise if I were you," I replied. "Besides, as stubborn as you are, you'll probably get your way."

She cried.

"But I'm stubborn too, Grandma," I amended.

There was no merciful hand to ease her suffering as she had ended the life of a small rabbit all those years ago.

A few months later when Grandma got her wish, no one held my hand as I took my last look. But as we waited for the minister to begin the service, Mom leaned over and whispered in my ear.

"No more nickels," she said.

© Tony Bender, 1992

Rusted Machinery

He came from an era of dust bowls and bankruptcies and it forever changed his view of the world. Not that his world was all that big. It didn't extend much past the city borders of Ashley, ND.

He and Grandma started out back then with a cow and a borrowed $20 bill. Well, this ain't no fairy tale. They went broke and had to start all over again a couple years later. So he knew the value of a dollar and spent the rest of his life scrimping and saving, scarred by the helplessness of having none.

His head shook disapprovingly when he asked and found out how much my new Mustang cost. Everything I bought was sure to be greeted by a similar response. "That's a lot of money!"

So I should have known the end was near when The Redhead and I went to visit him at the nursing home in Ashley last month. We brought in Duck, our four-month old brittany spaniel. Grandpa looked down approvingly from his wheelchair as Duck sat patiently, letting his head be scratched. "He's a good dog. What did you pay?"

I was afraid to tell him—$250—but he just nodded. "That's not too bad," he said. I almost fell out of my chair. Either Grandpa was getting soft, or he just liked dogs more than I remembered.

It was his birthday—his 85th—and he proudly showed me

the birthday card from President Clinton, tucked safely away in his drawer. "That was nice," I said as I eyed the print-shop signature. The Redhead agreed it was indeed thoughtful of our President to remember Grandpa's birthday.

Grandpa looked thin, his thick-knuckled, gnarled farmer's hands, large and out of proportion to his thin wrists. He patted the armrest of the wheelchair. "My legs are done," he said matter-of-factly. "I won't walk no more."

He wasn't angry. Not bitter. Just accepting of the passage of time. That's the way he was, the most easy-going fellow I'd known. He just never seemed to get angry—even under verbal attack from Grandma. He'd just shrug his shoulders and wait till Cyclone Bertha blew over. While he worked hard through his life on the farm, emotionally, he just seemed to float unconcerned through it all.

As we sat there in his room, my mind slipped back five years to a Sunday when Grandpa and I had been driving around Ashley, talking and looking. He had asked me to pull over by an old building that had some rusting machinery beside it.

As we walked, he told me the history of the decaying building and the machinery. He'd been a young man when the building had been hammered together. It caused him to reflect. Machinery that once was state-of-the-art now rusted before him. I suppose he couldn't help but feel a little useless and alone.

"I'm gonna go until I'm 85—then that's enough," he declared. I kidded him about that. Imagine just being able to choose your own time. But that was just like Grandpa. Selfishly, I hoped he was wrong.

When the attendant came to get Grandpa for dinner, we stalled. But Grandpa was hungry, so after a few more minutes I wheeled him to a table with some other rusting old machines.

I surveyed the group dubiously. "You sure you, want to sit here? Looks like a pretty rough crew," I added boisterously— to the pleasure of the old men.

I made sure to let everyone know, just as loudly, that Grandpa was celebrating his birthday. Grandpa lit up like a birthday candle. Said he was gonna make 85. By gum, he had, hadn't he?

That's how I left him.

In my heart, I wasn't really surprised to hear that he'd died in his sleep last Sunday. Like he'd happily floated through life, he just drifted away peacefully.

I'll miss that old man.

© Tony Bender, 1995

Letter to Mike

Dear Michael,

First of all, I know that you would rather be called Mike. I called you Michael for so many years before you asserted that it was Mike. You have trained me well, and I haven't called you Michael for a long time. It is because you have grown up enough to decide what you want to be called, that I feel the long version of your name fits you.

You've grown up in so many ways that it's taken me by surprise. I see you thinking so many serious private thoughts.

Brooding is a word that comes to mind, but when I think of your good nature that doesn't seem possible.

I have been meaning to write this for some time now, but I put it off because I knew it would turn me into a blubbering fool.

I cleaned out my car the other day and discovered one of your drawings. I hung it in the place where all great primitives go—the refrigerator.

I have every letter you sent me. A favorite came with the newspaper clipping of you and your championship basketball team. "We won," it said.

I was so proud. I still am.

Part of the inspiration for what I write here at 4 a.m. came from a talk I had with a young woman this summer. She met me and exclaimed as most of your friends do,"You're Mike's brother!"

She has a special brother, too, and she told me about her protective spirit when he gets teased for being slow and different. I understood perfectly. I was your protector when I still lived at home. The occasions for my services were few. You were so loved and accepted. You still are.

Everywhere we go, somebody knows you. You could get elected.

Because you were special, you had everyone in the family in the palm of your hand. It used to drive me crazy, and I tried to fill the role of disciplinarian. I was secretly pleased that you would listen to me with no questions asked. You knew I meant business. Alas, that role is another one for which there is no longer a need. You have a job now and an apartment. And you're as free with your money as I was at your age.

You have awakened to the world. I hear you talk about grown up things like cars and girl friends. You play your snare drum daily in your quest for rock n' roll stardom.

I will never discourage your vision. I will never say no. Anything is possible if we try hard. God is surely on your side. Keep on believing.

You have a lot going for you. Many of your special friends were hidden away by families who were embarrassed that they were special. You have marched by our side, and we are proud to have you there.

As much as you were spoiled, we have been spoiled worse by having you in our lives. We have an exclusive club. We are all loved by you. When we hurt, you make us feel better.

You are so perceptive. You can spot a heartache a mile

away.

I wouldn't trade you for a thousand perfect brothers. For one thing, it would be too dang crowded around the table.

Well Mike, I don't know if this letter will help you in your struggles to overcome that invisible cage that holds you down sometimes. I don't know if it will change the times when you can't do things or go places because your freedom is not complete.

But Mike, remember this, your spirit is free, and it can go places that your body cannot take you.

There is your advantage.

I see that as clearly as you read our hearts.

I never told you this, Mike, but whenever people ask about you, this is what I say: "He has the purest soul of anyone I've ever known."

Your Big Brother,
Tony

Writer's note: Mike Bender is 32, employed at 3-M and recently moved into his own home. He's doing just fine. Mike has William's Syndrome.

Don't be Lost, Daddy

Blessed are the divine moments of clarity. Blessed and rare as the balance we seek in our lives.

The holidays are hectic in the newspaper business. *Every* week is hectic in the newspaper business, but the holiday season forces us into road gear.

Around Thanksgiving we disappear behind computer screens. In mid-January we will emerge. Until I became a husband and a father, balance didn't seem so important.

The late nights and the weekends at the office take a toll on me, I know. But I didn't recognize the toll it takes on those around me—until my two-year-old son set me straight.

I should have understood the message earlier. His grandparents thought it was funny, when Dylan rebuffed Grandpa Gary. Dylan didn't have time to play, he informed them. "I have to write my column."

I frowned when the story was told to me, a "Cat's in the Cradle" father.

Sure, it was a little cute and a little flattering when he perched at my desk and pounded the computer keys. When I'd peek in and ask, "What are you doing?" he would respond, "Working."

I should have seen the signs. The more time I stole from him, the more unruly he became. He set a record for "time out" in December. He's the Mark McGwire of time out.

One morning, as I struggled to get his coat and boots on for the ride to daycare, he wriggled and fussed, kicking off his boots as fast as I could get them on. It was great fun for him, but I was running late and I lost my temper. Finally, I threw him over my shoulder, grabbed his coat and boots and stomped toward the door, "Fine, I'll take you like this!" Of course, his mother stepped in and helped me get him dressed. "He wants so desperately to play with you," she admonished.

When we pulled up to the daycare, I apologized. He still had tears in his eyes. "I'm sorry, Dylan. Daddy was naughty. I'm sorry I lost my temper..."

Sweetly, he offered to help me find it.

Last week, we were painting interior walls in anticipation of hosting Christmas. On Monday, while The Redhead was working late, I painted while Dylan parked in front of our new babysitter, Scooby Doo.

On my way outside to fetch the ladder, I informed him. "Stay right here, Dylan. I'm going out for a minute but I'll be right back."

He nodded. Listened intently.

Later, as I was touching up in the kitchen, Dylan stepped up to me. "Daddy, don't be lost. I'm going downstairs for my toys. But I'll be right back."

That really hit me. *Daddy, don't be lost.*

It occurred to me that I had been lost.

Lost in my work.

Lost in self-absorption.

Just lost.

I've been trying harder. But enlightenment can be fleeting and once in a while The Redhead has to remind me, "Don't be lost, Daddy."

The other night, Dylan asked if he could play with his toys on the coffee table.

I looked up from my magazine. "Sure, Dylan."

"He wants *you* to play with him," our interpreter interrupted.

When I dropped to the floor, Dylan leaned against me as we quietly maneuvered plastic figures around the table. As he snuggled against me, I kissed his head.

It's so easy to get lost.

© Tony Bender, 1998

Tech Support

Dylan came ripping around the coffee table, tripped on the cord and our Macintosh laptop crashed to the floor.

He apologized, but he still wouldn't come up with the $600 it would cost to put in a new motherboard.

Six hundred dollars! That's what they told me when I called a Bismarck repair shop. I got the same response when I called Rapid City.

So I called my insurance agent. Nope, it wasn't covered. He mentioned some technicality relating to Jupiter's alignment with Mars on the Thursday I signed the policy.

"So what you're telling me is I have a wonderful, almost affordable insurance policy, but if I actually hope to have anything covered, I need to spend more on insurance."

"Yes," he confessed, stunned that I had uncovered the scam. That leaves me one for three with the insurance company on computer disasters.

When we moved two years ago, my laser printer was damaged. Foolishly, I told the truth. I wasn't exactly sure how it happened. Well, without witnesses, filmed coverage and a notary, my policy wouldn't cover the $1,000 loss.

They did cover the loss of a computer that was a victim of a lightning strike—but only because the pile of cinders was still smoking when the insurance adjuster stopped in.

Desperate, and not quite ready to toss my laptop on the pile with all the other uninsured wrecks, I found an ad in my MacWorld magazine.

I checked out the web site, and they looked like a reputable repair shop. Endorsed by Apple and everything.

Well, they patched me into Brian in tech support.

Brian is a typical geek. Just like the math wiz in high school with a pocket protector and a permanent wedgie, Brian snorts a sort of superiority snort because your disaster is child's play for him.

I described the damage.

"Snort! Motherboard's shot!"

"Yeah, Two places told me that."

This got Brian all excited. "Snort. So tell me how much they wanted to fix it."

"Six hundred dollars!"

"SNORT!!! I'll fix it for $150! Snort! Snort."

I could almost see him doing his superiority snort dance.

I half-expected never to see the computer again (in which case it would be theft and clearly not covered under the terms of my insurance policy), but less than 10 days later my computer was back, spit-polished and running like a dream. I paid the $150 and made Dylan sign an IOU.

When the "clicker" on the touch pad wore out I called Brian.

"Hey Brian, I need to send you my laptop again."

I described the problem.

"SNORT!!! You can fix that yourself. I'll send you the part for $15."

"Are you sure I can do it myself?"

Brian snorted supportively and assured me that untrained

raccoons have successfully completed the task under laboratory conditions.

When the part arrived, I confidently dismantled the laptop. But after staring at the maze of solder and computer chips for 15 minutes, I got on the hotline.

"I'm sorry, Brian isn't in today."

"Uhhh, You got a raccoon?"

Instead they put me in touch with another guy in tech support. Dave didn't snort and was altogether serious.

I described the operation.

"You shouldn't be doing that! You should have sent it in."

"Yeah but..."

Dave was taking no guff. "Listen mister, let me ask you something. You have black circles around your eyes?"

"Noooo..."

"You have a brown and black bushy, striped tail?"

"Well, nooo."

"Well then, you are not qualified to install a clicker."

I could have ratted out Brian, but anyone who saves me $450 deserves a little loyalty.

"Look, Dave, I begged. I've got computer innards scattered all over my wife's desk and I'm in over my head..."

Dave was merciful. In ten minutes the computer was reassembled with a successful clicker transplant.

The experience only gave me more confidence. Since then, Brian has walked me through two hard drive installations and a power supply replacement. And we're not telling Dave.

Snort.

© Tony Bender, 2000

Preachers Meeting

"What do they want?" The Redhead asked.

I didn't know. But having the ministerial association request you meet with them can induce a fair amount of nervousness.

As an adult, there's a certain confidence that comes with the knowledge that you can't get sent to the principal's office anymore. This was like being summoned to the big principal's office in the sky.

Tuesday's were out, I told the good Reverend. Layout day. Gotta get the paper out.

OK, he would get back to me.

Whew, a reprieve.

A few weeks later, he called. "How about Thursdays?"

"Thursdays are good," I replied finally, after searching fruitlessly for some sort of prior engagement.

"So are you planning an exorcism?" I queried.

"Do we need to?" he countered.

In the weeks before the meeting, I started a mental tally of recent sins I might have to explain:

• Mentioned beer in my column a couple times.

• Made fun of Jimmy Swaggart.

• Voted for a Democrat.

• Fibbed about how much I liked The Redhead's meatloaf.

- Cruised Main with Alice Cooper blaring on the stereo.
- Used a word defining a beast of burden inappropriately in a column about politicians.
- Omitted the church directory from the newspaper a couple of times. Legions of little old ladies come in to shake their fingers at me when that happens. The only thing that made them madder was when we were a week late with coverage of the big hat show. We lost three subscribers, and someone put a potato in my tailpipe.

For any editor, deciding what goes into the paper and what won't fit, is a daunting challenge. Sometimes a last-minute ad or important news item walks through the door, and you have to decide what gets bumped. Pull the community social column and you're a dead man.

You might not think its important that Hulda and Beezer visited Shorty and Bertha, that Hulda wore her blue flannel dress and that Bertha poured tea and served kuchen, but miss something like that, and they'll make the Hat Show Massacre look like a minor skirmish.

So some weeks I rationalize that everyone knows when their church service is. But not everyone knows that Duke's Full Service has snow tires on sale. Snow tires will allow parishioners to get to church safely, I convince myself. I'm pretty sure that Moses, Abraham and all those other Bible guys would handle it the same way.

Of course, the thought of explaining my rationale to the God Squad had me reconsidering the validity of my logic.

As I walked to the door for the morning meeting, I was getting into the spirit of things, singing "Old Time Religion." Actually, it was sort of a medley.

Give me that old time religion,

Shake it up baby, now,
Give me that old time religion,
Twist and Shout!

The meeting went pretty well. There was no smiting or anything. We had coffee and rolls—which might explain the origin of the term, holy roller.

They're pretty good guys, I decided. And when they asked me about some modifications to my church page policy, I folded like a wet newspaper.

Hey, the last thing a guy needs is a plague of warthogs or something tromping through the office. I mean, I'd like to think the Lord is a pretty patient guy and has a good sense of humor, but why risk wrath and smiting and brimstone and stuff?

I would try to do better, I vowed. But if it comes down to a hat show or the church directory, the hat show is going in. Some of those hat show ladies can get downright medieval.

I think God will understand.

© Tony Bender, 1998

Loons in the Kitchen

For the first time in our brief marriage, The Redhead and I find ourselves living in a house.

Gone are the noisy college kids we had for neighbors just a few short months ago. Parking is no longer an irritation.

Yes, the privacy of a home is certainly a wonderful thing. We've been able to unpack boxes that haven't been open in years. Wedding gifts that remained packaged are now in use. We're comfortable.

When we moved in, I negotiated what I believed to be a reasonable agreement. She gets to decorate the entire house; I get to decorate my office.

Naturally, she stole all the good stuff, so I've been left with a vintage Roadrunner poster, a hand-painted moose on a piece of driftwood and a mirror advertising cheap brandy.

Eventually, armed with the obvious evidence of my poorly-decorated office, she will demand to decorate it herself, thereby violating another of the many treaties we have had, and I will be saddled with frills and pastels.

We were in the house roughly 13 seconds when The Redhead declared that the shiny white paneling on the kitchen wall would simply have to go. Seems she had similar walls to wash daily back on her parents' dairy farm in Verona.
It wasn't a happy memory.

There was no way she would stand for a kitchen that reminded her of a dairy barn.

Wallpaper was just the ticket. "OK," I said, "but it's got to be something subtle." She smiled sweetly and agreed.

Subtle is a relative term.

When she returned from her business trip later that week, she brought with her the subtle wallpaper. However the 'subtle' country pattern was accompanied by a bold green and maroon vertically striped paper that was to run up about three feet off the floor, where it would dramatically clash with the subtle paper.

Sort of a Volkswagen meets Mack Truck motif.

But there was more. She'd purchased a matching border with ducks on it, she said.

I was skeptical, but I decided to wait and see.

When I returned from work, I have to admit it looked good. But those weren't ducks on the wall.

"What did you say those birds were again?" I asked.

"Some goose or something," she responded from the hall. "Why?"

"Well, honey, we have *loons* in our kitchen."

"Well, I'm used to that," she said.

I should have known it wouldn't end there. The next time I came home, we had green and blue doors—blue to bring out the subtle blue in the wallpaper. I didn't fuss too much. It wasn't like she was expecting *me* to paint or wallpaper.

But when she started talking about painting the living room, I protested. It's white and I like white. So we compromised. She could do the hall. When she came back from the hardware store—where I'm sure Dave is planning a lavish retirement based on her estimated annual purchases—she had two paints

—'pollen' and 'pottery.' An Aztec border would compliment the two, she assured me.

I came home that evening to tumult. I had a screaming yellow hallway. It was the shade of yellow that triggers epileptic fits. It was complimented by yellow paw prints on the carpet. When I coaxed my banished dog from beneath the bed, I found a sad-eyed, yellow-eared, yellow-tailed Brittany.

Still, I remained strangely serene—in a state of mind I suppose you'd have upon meeting aliens for the first time.

"What do you think?" The Redhead asked cautiously.

I was silent for a very long time as I searched carefully for the words. "I still love you, Honey," I said as I gave her a big hug.

And then I went out to the kitchen to admire the loons.

© Tony Bender, 1995

I Was Tricked

I'm not proud that I violated my wedding vows. Maybe I was just too naive and unrealistic. Right after the part about promising "to be square and obey the law of the pack," I interjected a solemn promise "never to paint, wallpaper or fix anything remotely mechanical around the house unless it directly pertains to football."

For instance, just days before the Super Bowl, I discovered that my DSS receiver was on the blink. So I was forced to disconnect it and hook up another one. Perfectly within the rules. On occasion, I have wired speakers to get that surround sound for big games. Again, completely legal.

But the part about painting and wallpapering...I was tricked, I say. Tricked! I tried explaining that to Harley, Mitch and Darren over lunch at the Prairie Winds Restaurant the other day. We were sitting around discussing guy things—forklifts and such—when the topic got to the past weekend's activities. "I was painting," I volunteered.

Forks stopped in mid air. It went as silent as it does when Clint Eastwood walks into the saloon. A man at the next table gasped audibly and covered his young son's ears. Harley and Mitch eyed me suspiciously. Darren fainted into his knepfla soup.

"You didn't paint with *your wife* did you?" Mitch asked.

"Well... I had to," I explained lamely.

Harley shook his head in disgust. "No good can come from that."

"Once, my wife asked me if I liked the new wallpaper," Mitch recounted, "and after I told her I did, she tore it down."

Everyone at the table nodded sagely in unison.

"At least you didn't help her wallpaper," Mitch said.

"Well... I..."

They never let me finish. Mitch gave me a disgusted look and moved to another table. Harley dragged away Darren, who had a wax bean lodged in his nostril.

Like I said, I was tricked. Like all women, The Redhead is roughly 723 times smarter than me. Picture Einstein and Dorf at a chess board and you have the picture.

She started setting me up at the wallpaper display when she pretended to let me have a choice in wallpaper—after making a widely circuitous route around the stuff with fighter planes or dairy cows on it.

"Which one do you like?" she asked, holding out two identical rolls.

"They look the same to me," I answered, bewildered.

She assured me they were completely different.

"I dunno. That one?"

She smiled knowingly, put the one I had picked back on the shelf, and condescendingly pinched my cheek like your old Aunt Hilda did when you were a kid.

She never said a word about me helping.

But she did let me know what a big, strong, handsome and able man I was, several times in the days approaching the week-end. And she made it a point to start the project when I was in the house.

When she told me she planned to start in the corner—the

141

temptress—I couldn't contain myself. "You have to drop a plumb line in the middle of the wall and work to the corners," I explained like a big, strong, handsome, able man.

"Well, if you're so smart, "then you can help," she retorted. Like I said, I was tricked. (Guy Rule #17: Never be right about anything.) We did get the paper up but it took three marital counseling sessions down at the lumber yard—it's a new service—before our marriage recovered. As Zeke, our counselor, explained to The Redhead, as I stared meekly at my shoes, "Guys don't know no better."

But I should have known better. I'm still paying for the last time I offered advice. About a year ago, I had the audacity to suggest that we needed to modify Dylan's bedtime routine. He kept weaseling his way into our bed or demanding we stay in his room until he was asleep. "Gotta put our foot down," said I.

To The Redhead, my suggestion was a heinous affront to Motherhood and all that is good and just in the world. Since I was such a child care genius, she told me, I could be in charge of Dylan's nighttime care. Now, if he wakes up with a cold, I get up with him. Even if The Redhead hears him first at 3 a.m., she elbows me awake: "Hey Mary Poppins, your kid needs you."

The Viet Cong used the same techniques at the Hanoi Hilton. First comes sleep deprivation and the next thing you know you're chanting slogans for Uncle Ho. Or wallpapering. Or painting.

I'm not particularly proud of it, but I even replaced a door knob the other day. I held out for weeks though. At first, you had to turn it just right to open it. Then the inside knob fell off completely. I called it our Hotel California door because "You can never leave."

Actually, I didn't mind using the basement window to get in and out for a few days. Guys are adaptable. However, when the entire assembly fell off, I was forced into action.

I'm not proud of fixing the door, but I did get out of a good half hour of painting.

A Man in my Bed

Ifound another man in my bed last night, and it's not the first time.

He's short. A little taller than Danny DiVito but better looking. And the Redhead makes no bones about it; he's her favorite.

When, I wonder, did I fall so far in the rankings? I used to be number one. She used to hang on every inane word, smile at my silly jokes and fawn over me.

Now this other guy has taken over and while I remain well entrenched in popularity above the family dog, I am clearly numero deuce.

And I have become complacent. I usually wait until he's asleep before I carry him to his room. But last night, while his beloved Mama slumbered peacefully, Dylan was comfortably ensconced in my spot, watching Cartoon Network. It was 9:30 p.m. Doesn't Scooby ever sleep?

Dylan looked up and in no uncertain terms told me to go sleep elsewhere. *He* would sleep with Mommy from now on.

It had already been a long day, and I wasn't up for a frontal assault, so I figured I'd camp out downstairs for 20 minutes until he fell asleep. Then I'd toss his little butt into his own bed.

So I feigned hurt feelings and shuffled away.

The boy adores his Mama and she loves him right back

twice as much. One day, as he declared his allegiance to her forever, she smiled knowingly. "Well Sweetie, someday you'll be a teenager and you'll hang out with your friends and you won't want anything to do with your Mama."

"I don't want to be a teenager!" Dylan wailed, envisioning a transformation every bit as awful as Jeff Goldblum's in *The Fly.* "I love my Mama!"

My relationship with the boy is a little more complex. I'm the drill sergeant, always threatening dire consequences—like revoking his chocolate milk privileges and other heinous tortures.

Still we're buddies. We fish together, and I'm considering letting Dylan use real hooks this year. Consider yourself warned.

Just between you and me, I like it when I have the boy all to myself. Cuz when Mom is not in the house, Daddy-O is the coolest cat you ever saw.

According to a long-standing treaty with The Redhead, she gets up with the boy at the crack of dawn and in return, I have the bedtime routine.

Unless I am covering a city council meeting or some other exciting evening endeavor, at 8 p.m., I herd Dylan to his room.

One glass of water.

Check.

One Flintstones vitamin.

Check.

Special blue blankie.

Check.

Stuffed yellow beaver.

Check.

Last minute potty break.

145

Check.

Then Dylan picks out the evening's literary selection. Sometimes we read about Power Rangers. Sometimes it's Bert and Ernie, and lots of times it's Dr. Seuss. Daddy is a top-notch Dr. Seuss reader. While I read, Dylan snuggles close. And without fail, despite leaden eyelids, he always demands another book. By this time it's nearly midnight.

Generally, he stages a jailbreak or two to hug his Mommy. It's quite a routine those two have. He'll be giving her one of those special "giant hugs" when I come in to haul his keister back to bed. As I carry him away, he half-heartedly cries, "Mama!" while stretching his arms out toward her, pretending it's some sort of final goodbye.

And, on cue, she stretches her arms out while remaining propped on pillows. "Dylan," she moans. She'll miss him. But not enough to get out from under the quilt. They both grin mischievously at their little joke. And I smile, too.

I was paging through the *Sporting News* when Dylan came downstairs after my banishment.

"Daddy, I'm sorry I told you to go away. Can you come up and read me a book?"

"You bet," I say clicking off the lights. "I would love to read my favorite boy a book."

We hug when I'm done reading, and I tuck him in.

"And remember..."

"Don't let the bedbugs bite," he finishes with a giggle.

I am at the doorway before I turn in the dim light.

"I love you, buddy."

"I love you, too, Daddy," he chirps.

We both sleep well.

© Tony Bender, 2000

146

The Brick

I have an old brick in my home that I use as a door-stop. It is dusty tan and worthless in a monetary sense.

But for me, it binds me to my heritage, to a past where a bigger-than-life great-grandfather walked and worked a Dakotah homestead.

I know him only through my grandfather's memories and my mother's recollections, but part of what he was, I am.

He came from Russia in the early days of the century, leaving a home that had become oppressive, a country that stole young men for the army never to be seen again.

My great-grandfather saw his brothers disappearing and wanted better for his sons. So he sold everything he owned and quietly slipped away to the Black Sea city of Odessa and boarded the ship that would bring them to America.

In America men were free, land was free and any hard-working man could raise a family in dignity. He went where other Russian immigrants had settled—North Dakota.

Hearing of an unclaimed quarter of land, he walked some 40 miles cross-country with just a loaf of bread.

When he found the spot, south of Gackle, it was nothing but buffalo grass and rocks, but with strong hands he built a home.

It weathered many brutal winters and sweltering summers and it molded my grandfather, a son of the prairie. He, in turn, molded my mother who molded me.

My grandfather recalls a time—he was just a boy—when slippery con-men preyed on the Russian innocents. They would observe a farmer buying a piece of equipment with cash and later would pretend to represent the seller. The shyster would demand payment and more often than not would get it from the honest men who had been scarred by the Czar's regime and the Bolshiveks who followed. It was easy to oppress men who were trained to be trod upon.

One day such a man came to the homestead. "What does he want?" my great-grandfather asked his son. My grandfather was the interpreter for his father who spoke only Russian.

"He wants you to pay for the reaper," the son told the father who replied that he had—in hard cash.

"Then where is the receipt?" the con-man asked.

My great-grandfather stepped inside the barn and produced the receipt—masquerading in the guise of a three-pronged pitchfork.

That was good enough, and the man ran for his life.

I thought about that one spring when my grandfather took me to that long-abandoned homestead. It was sunny and only a hint of wind whistled as cattle drank at the water tank that marked the site of his roots. We walked the pasture and found the rusty, paper-thin steel that had once been the fender of his old Model T. The house was nothing but a depression in the ground surrounded by weeds and some dying trees. As I kicked the dirt unconsciously in contemplation, I uncovered a muddy brick that my great-grandfather had once handled.

My mother tells of the quiet man who lived in their home in later years. The man who walked a lot and held his grandchildrens' hands.

I never knew the man.

That brick is all I have.

A reminder of memories that are not mine.

This morning, I stubbed my toe on that brick in the bumbling moments of dawn.

The pain was dulled by sleepiness, and instead of cursing, I managed a small smile as I remembered the pitchfork and the man I never knew.

© Tony Bender, 1992

A New Tacklebox

The gleaming tan and green tacklebox beckoned. It was on sale. I'd never actually bought a tacklebox before. The two tackleboxes I'd owned before had been hand-me-downs from my father.

The first was a small, steel box, spray painted green to hide the scars. I used it for years. But somewhere along the miles of my life, it was discarded.

The tacklebox I'd been using until this year was my father's last one. It rested, dusty and spotted by oil, in the garage after his death, so I took it home with me.

It was bursting with tackle. Hooks and rigs for every type of freshwater fish in the Midwest. The irony of this impressive collection did not escape me. I smiled. I chuckled. You see, my father, the man with this intimidating tangle of spinners, daredevils, bobbers and lead weights, rarely fished.

I think we fished together—maybe a half dozen times. There just never seemed to be enough time.

But the tacklebox spoke volumes about Dad's optimism. One day he would fish for weeks on end. He would snag dozens of hooks on sunken logs. Lunkers would snap leaders. And he would be prepared.

I took that tacklebox with me every year on my annual fishin' trip with The Boys up on the Continental Divide of Colorado. But when I added my trout gear to the box, it began to bulge.

A search for a #10 snelled hook could last minutes.

Like my father, I could not pass by the aisles of fishing gear without purchasing some new wonder bait or guaranteed spinner. So I bought the gigantic new tacklebox. It boasted drawers and compartments enough for two fishermen.

I waited till the last day before I was to leave on this men-only trip to transfer the gear from Dad's old tacklebox to my new one. I didn't expect it to become a ritual, but it did as I lovingly stored all of my father's paraphernalia.

The Redhead urged me to finish the task. It was her last chance to get some work out of me for a week. But the ritual had become religion and each hook safely stored, a prayer.

I tucked the old, empty tacklebox into the closet. The Redhead plans to use it to decorate Dylan's room. And when he is older, it will go back into service.

The Boys found a new lake this year. Surrounded by fragrant pines and crumbling granite mountains, the waters gleamed as flawless as a mirror in the orangish early morning light. As we sat on the shore in dawn's radiant silence, two moose emerged from the shadowed forest and splashed noisily across the lake to graze choice rushes. As we watched, Bob spoke inspired words. "This is good for the soul." Fishing is religion.

Fishing was fair—better than last year—and I was the leading fisherman. On the last day, when our luck had run out, I reeled in my line. Then I felt a tug. Surprised, I didn't set the hook well. I reeled the 10 inch trout closer to shore, and he darted bravely between the rocks, fighting for his life. Then, as Tom lowered the net, the fish slipped off the hook. Tom strained to find the fish, hoping to net him before he reached deeper water. Silently, curiously, I cheered for the trout. With a sassy swish of his tail and a last sparkling gleam of rainbow scales, he disappeared.

I packed my gear. I felt a few pangs of guilt as I glanced at that new tacklebox, as if leaving that old tacklebox behind had been a betrayal. But I silenced the guilt with my rationalizations. The many remaining empty drawers are a testament to *my* optimism. I will fill them. And I will fish.

Dad, your tacklebox didn't make the trip this year.

But you did.

© Tony Bender, 1997

Writer's note: This summer, we bought Dylan a   new fishing rod, and I gave him my father's old tacklebox.

Wally's World

"**N**ow I don't need no advertisin'," he says as he opens the door to his shop. "It's just a hobby for me now. Don't need no ads."

"Hey, Wally, it's an interview. Won't cost you a cent."

"Better not."

To the sportsmen and women of Adams County, Wally Springer don't need no advertisin'. The 83-year-old gunsmith's work is legend, so good in fact, the Shah of Iran once commissioned a half dozen Springer Originals.

He's the last of a dying breed, a craftsman—an artist. "An artist paints it in his mind first," Wally says, his rough-hewn hands spread wide in explanation. "It's the same with a gunsmith."

In his shop, sawdust prevails as blocks of walnut wait to be transformed. Rifles of various make and caliber crowd the gun rack and a master's tools await his hand. This is Wally's world.

Wally has called this area home since 1925. "My folks homesteaded down south of Slim Buttes." The lineage has taken root, and Wally and his wife, Bernadine, produced nine children with locales so diverse, Wally has trouble remembering who's married to whom and who lives where. "The last three-four years, my memory ain't what it used to be," he admits.

But he hasn't forgotten what has made him a local treasure. His hands and mind still turn a cacophony of power tools into a symphony of polished steel and gleaming wood. He's hard pressed to explain his talent. "All my life, just had a knack for things. I found I could take a block of wood and make a stock. I was born with it. You have to be born with it," he offers.

All the hunters know is, he's a great one.

Somewhere, there's a former governor of North Dakota with a Springer rifle, Wally can't quite place the name, he tells you from under his NRA cap. The guy couldn't have been that important... And the Shah, "He was over to see those American doctors," he recounts. The Peacock Throne was looking for the best rifles to take home. "We got the job," Wally says. We was Wally and Adam Lefor from Dickinson, an ivory artist who inlaid carvings into Wally's rosewood and walnut stocks.

To build a great rifle, "You have to understand a firearm's capabilities," Wally says. You have to know your powder, he adds. "You see, your hand loads are better than factory. You load for a very specific use."

It helps to be a marksman. And Wally is not shy about telling you about his place among the great shooters. "I'm the best," he says in his knowing matter-of-fact style. "I've shot rams at 700-750 yards. I'm an expert rifleman.

"I've shot moose in Canada, caribou in the Arctic and the Dahl Ram—that was in Whitehorse," (Yukon Territory). Many coyotes have suffered under the business end of a Springer rifle, and Wally spent more than a few hours in his plane picking them off.

Through it all, Wally says he's never had anything that he considered a close call. "I don't know. I've been real close to bears—to a grizzly. They come at you with their mouth wide open, screaming. They sound like a mad horse."

One Wally shot at 300 yards; the other was a wounded, raging grizzly that came after him and his hunting partner, who had misplaced the bullet. Now c'mon, Wally, when that bear got within 30 yards, didn't your hands start shaking? "No," Wally says. "I never get afraid. I knew he didn't have a chance." And the bear isn't here to tell his side of the story, so Wally's word is law on the matter.

This is Wally's world.

In Wally's world the fall air is crisp; the deer are fat; pheasants plentiful. Hunters can thank Wally's father, John Albert Springer, who was one of the first to introduce pheasants to the area. They have been fruitful, and Wally promises a good year for sportsmen. Hunting will be "Good, very good. Very, very good. Deer hunting and pheasants—probably as good as there is in the U.S. It's going to be good this fall."

But Wally won't be out this year. It's a concession to age and the ravages of time. A concession to the loss of his right eye 17 years ago, when a rifle exploded in his face. "It was a freak accident. Very freak. It just did it. That's all. That piece of brass is still in my eye."

Wally brings out the pieces of the shell that took his shooting eye. He lost depth perception and gained a conversation piece. "I'm getting along okay without it," Wally asserts. But he acknowledges that it was a challenge to learn to shoot left-handed, with his other eye. "It took me quite a while. I wasn't as good.

"This finger is educated," he explains as he holds up the Springer trigger finger. "You don't have to tell it to pull the trigger." Teaching his other finger what the original trigger finger had learned in a lifetime was hard, "but I don't give up easy." But is he still the best triggerman around? Why ask? You know the answer.

155

You want to learn to shoot? Go to the mountain. "Learn from an oldtimer like me," Wally says. "Are there many old-timers like me? No, there aren't," he answers.

And you know he's right.

© Tony Bender, 1994

Writer's note: Wally Springer died not long after I interviewed him.

Anvil and Forge

Most days Lloyd Bjella opens the door to Epping Iron Works and walks to the forge that warmed his feet as a child.

Stepping through the door transports him to a world that existed 50 years ago.

Here time stands still.

An old trip hammer poses in the spot it did half a century ago. It still pounds metal with the same bell-ringing ferocity it did when it was new.

"I grew up in the shop," Bjella says. A tattered old photo shows two-year-old Lloyd in a white suit standing on the anvil in his father, Asle's, shop. Asle had dirtied the garment as he lifted the child to the top of the anvil.

"Mother gave him particular hell because his black hands soiled my white suit," Lloyd says. Eighty-one years later, Lloyd picks up the four-pound hammer he uses to pound wayward metal into shape at the same old anvil.

Old-fashioned plowshares come from as far away as Canada and Minnesota to be sharpened by his hands. "You've gotta have just the right shape to it in order to plow," he says as he eyes his handiwork.

The trip hammer does the final chore of sharpening the blade. In the beginning, it was a two-man project. "What a terrible job," Bjella says. The shares, which break the ground, are

157

bolted on to the moldboards—the curved blade that rolls the soil over. The old-style plowshares have been replaced for the most part by the disposable kind—the kind that don't require sharpening. Still, some farmers cling stubbornly to the old-style shares that can be sharpened time and time again.

But those old-fashioned shares and those old-fashioned farmers are fading away. With them goes the art of black-smithing. "The blacksmith shop is definitely on the way out. We all know that," says Bjella. "But there's still a call once in awhile for the big forge and the anvil."

When Asle Bjella established the shop in 1906, shortly after his arrival from Norway, there were many calls. Plowshares had to be sharpened, wagon wheels needed fixing and horses needed shoes. "I shod a lot of horses," Lloyd says. "The broncs were ornery, but those big farm draft horses would get sleepy or tired and start to lean on you. It was heavy to hold that leg up."

Even today, hundreds of cattle in the area wear brands made by Bjella. "After I've made a brand, I put it on a nice piece of wood so I can see how it's gonna look on a critter," he says.

Lloyd became a full partner in the shop in 1941. "My father said, 'to make the transaction, it'll cost you a dollar,'" Lloyd recalls. "I didn't even have the dollar." The partnership lasted until 1961 when Asle died at the age of 84. "He worked in here till he passed away," Bjella says.

"He was a three-term legislator in the (North Dakota) House of Representatives," says Lloyd. Asle served at the capi-tal in the late 40s and early 50s, he adds. "He was too busy to campaign, so he put his card on the farmers' plowshares. "In those days we would have 200 plowshares lined up in here at one time," he says.

Epping was booming then, with a population topping 400.

Now there are maybe 50, says Bjella. While the number of plowshares has dwindled, like the people, to a spare few, Bjella still has his hands full fixing farm machinery in disrepair.

When the farmers are out in the fields, Bjella is busy in the shop with the massive arc welder. "There's nothing I enjoy more than fixing something from a farmer broke down in the field and get him going again," he says. "There's a lot of satisfaction in that—worth as much as the money you get for it."

Mention the cost of doing business, and Bjella may get rankled. The forge requires a special "smithing coal" that is specially mined and treated—with the sulfur removed. "It burns very hot. It's the only kind of coal that will work in a forge like that." The stuff costs about $300 a ton and is shipped out from mines in Virginia and Pennsylvania. "It's outrageous, but what are you gonna do? You can't operate without it, ya know."

Coal isn't the only product Bjella has brought in to keep the business going. The spokes and rims from buggies come from the Amish in Indiana. Bjella says there's a big call for wheelrights. His nephew, Greg Bjella, works in the shop during the summers putting wagon wheels together.

The orders are already filtering in, and Lloyd hopes Greg will be able to return from his new home in Anchorage, Alaska, to handle the wheel work this summer. One order came from Bob Walker in Montana, who had been driving his wagon in a recent Tom Cruise film, featuring a scene about the Oklahoma Land Rush. Walker called Lloyd and reported that when other wagons tipped over, the wheels were destroyed, and they were forced to pull out of the movie for lack of spares. Walker says his wagon tipped, but the wheels that Greg built held up.

It is Greg who will take over the shop when Lloyd is gone. "This is a three-generation thing now," says Lloyd.

Lloyd recalls a time when the shop would fix 40 wagon wheels "on a good day. In those days, everything was done by wagon," he says. "That gradually disappeared when the tractor started coming in and then the steam engine faded from the picture. I liked the days of the steam engine. Always did." He smiles at the memories filtering back.

He has no retirement plans. "I need something to do," he says. He adds that hanging on to the past in his blacksmith shop isn't a bad thing as long as there is a need.

"It's really part of this town's heritage," Bjella says. "If there ever was anything, this is it."

© Tony Bender, 1991

Pig Spleen Prediction

Everyone around here, it seems, wants to predict the weather.

There's a guy in Steele who makes his forecasts by looking at pig spleens.

For centuries, gypsies have used crystal balls to gaze into the future. In Steele, there's no need for all that technology. You just grab yourself a pig spleen and away you go.

The downside of using pig spleens is that recycling is pretty much out of the question. That is why you rarely see an ad in the classifieds under the heading, USED PIG INNARDS.

Now if I were a pig, this would be a real motivator for me to learn to talk like Arnold on Green Acres used to. That way when old Jed walks out to the barn wondering about the weather, Porky would just pipe up, "Gonna be colder than snot, Jed!" Then Jed could just hustle back to the house, call all the papers and make his report.

But until pigs can speak, things will get done the old fashioned way, and the only prediction of which the pigs can be certain is that a lot of them will be sacrificed in Steele in the name of science.

This strikes me as a terrible waste, and may I paraphrase, "a pig is a terrible thing to waste."

The Pork Council might want to look into promoting this

unique use for pigs: THE OTHER WHITE MEAT THAT WILL PREDICT THE WEATHER!

If this catches on it won't be long before world famous weathermen like Willard Scott and Jerry Bartz are slaying pigs on the evening news.

"Thank you, Monica. And now here's Jerry with this evening's pig sacrifice."

(Jerry reaches in and pulls out a bloody spleen.) "Guess what guys, it look's like rain!"

At this point, I know what you're wondering. You're wondering what the pig spleen in Steele said. And I'm going to tell you because I don't want all my readers going out and senselessly hacking up innocent swine just to figure it out.

So here's the deal... According to Jed in Steele, it's going to be a cold winter—the spleen came out bundled in a parka.

Hearing this prediction, heating oil and propane distributors immediately announced a winter shortage and hiked the price by 92 cents a gallon. Next time you drive by a refinery, throw your pig spleen at them.

What professionals like the Bureau of Weatherologists (BOW) say is remarkably similar to what Jed in Steele says, despite the fact that they rely on the highly advanced chicken gizzard method.

Once I sorted through all the scientific jargon, here's a summary of their report: Unlike El Nino, which brought milder temperatures to the northern plains last winter, a system of colder ocean water, La Nina, will cause colder weather in North Dakota. (La Nina, by the way, in English, means *poopy weather.* And for you history buffs, I believe La Nina was also the name of Sir Francis Drake's ship.)

Of course, asking a North Dakotan to relate to the concept

of *cold and colder* is a lot like asking them to distinguish the difference between *dead* as a door nail and *deader* than a door nail.

Also, BOW says our weather will be further complicated by La Bamba which will result in a deluge of dead Latin-American singers over the plains states.

Even my eternal contractor, Bill, predicts a cold winter based on the fact that the snow geese headed south early this year. Heck, I thought it was just because people were shooting at them.

And me? Despite the fact that I have no ready access to a pig spleen, I must concur with the other predictions.

I know it's going to be cold, because the night of the first frost, Little Man, our new 675 pound German wirehair, literally knocked down the front door to get in.

Add that to the fact that my Aunt Emma's mustache is extra thick and full this fall, and it does not bode well.

Bundle up.

© Tony Bender, 1998

Before Cholesterol

L ife used to be a lot easier. I can guarantee my Grandpa never had to worry about cholesterol. And he ate lard sandwiches for lunch almost every day. But that was before cholesterol was invented in the early eighties.

In Grandpa's day, a burger on the grill was just well-done, not teeming with carcinogens. And back then, three out of four doctors actually recommended smoking as the really cool thing to do. Although now, smoking may be making a comeback. I read somewhere that preliminary studies show smokers have a lower incidence of Parkinson's Disease and lungs.

Did you ever hear of your Grandma worrying about E-coli bacteria? Absolutely not! Heck, she used to thaw out the turkey on the counter a full week before Thanksgiving. So what if there is chicken blood on the knife? We can still use it to cut the birthday cake! Again, it was a simpler time, before E-coli was invented.

It wouldn't be so frustrating if these research geniuses could make up their minds. Things keep changing. Drinking alcohol used to be completely bad for you. But now, after studying the Italians and French, scientists have concluded they speak entirely different and weird languages. NO! HOLD IT! Actually, what they concluded was that in countries where red wine is swilled at every meal, the women are too juiced to shave their armpits. NO! NO! Really, what they figured out is these folks have virually no cholesterol and livers that resemble a three-day old tuna sandwich. You see, red wine kills cholesterol! (The way it works is, the cholesterol gets really tipsy, and then goes out driving curvy roads at a high rate of speed.)

In simpler times, if you ate plenty of lard, smoked regularly and drank lots of red wine, you ended up a 90-year-old forgetful old fart. Now, you get Alzheimer's.

Back in the good old days, prophets preached about the dangers of too much ozone in the ozone layer. Dentists encouraged patients to floss their teeth with asbestos.

Twenty years ago, sniffing radon gas was actually mandatory in seven states and legal in 13 others. Now you can only get it by prescription to combat hair loss.

Then, a few years later, in what may or may not have been a propaganda coup by the powerful lard industry, it was revealed that there is good cholesterol and bad cholesterol.

Sort of like there's good evil and bad evil.

So when the results of my first cholesterol test came back recently, I wasn't sure if the news was good or bad. All I'm going to say is the number was somewhere under 1,000.

When I called in, the nurse told me they found a whole cheese kuchen floating in my bloodstream. Not a good thing, she said.

But I guarantee you, in 10 years the New England Journal of Medicine is going to denounce fiber and recommend kuchen between meals.

Time is on my side.

© Tony Bender, 1999

The Rummage Sale

The Redhead loves rummage sales. So much she decided to have one of her own. Of course, like all important endeavors in our family, first we had a reasonable discussion. Then she did what she wanted to anyway.

We spent a full three weeks planning. We didn't discuss the prospect of parenthood that long.

Since my recovery from our first rummage sale, let me say now the whole rummage sale concept is clearly an insidious female plot to further subjugate men.

The Redhead began by pricing anything of mine that happened to be out of place—which was pretty much everything. So I was forced to buy much of my stuff back before the sale even started.

Then she made me go through all those (start the Twilight Zone music) boxes in the basement. Stuff I hadn't unpacked in the last six or seven moves.

We agreed on one thing. If we couldn't identify it, we'd sell it.

While sorting, The Redhead discovered two mice beneath the water heater. Since we are catless, I sigged the dog on them. Duck took one look and skulked upstairs. Some hunting dog.

So The Redhead used a golf club to scare them out. I wacked one with a hiking boot. The Redhead priced it at a dime and tossed it in a box.

The other one scurried up against her leg, quickly elevating her blood pressure. I haven't heard anything like that since my Slim Whitman album skipped. Doubled over in laughter, I was unable to kill the rodent.

Friday night, we hauled all our stuff to a friend's house in town where the sale was to be held.

I made it a point to price all the heavy stuff really cheap.

The sale was supposed to start at 9 a.m. but by 8 a.m., ladies on scouting missions cruised past like gang members in low riders. Others hovered across the street with binoculars. Gary Powers buzzed overhead in a U-2, having been called out of retirement by an enterprising rummager.

They gathered like the Sioux around Custer.

At 9 a.m. the horde swarmed over fences like Visigoths, elbowing like the Red Wings.

I cowered as ladies stacked piles of clothing in their arms.

Later, The Redhead explained that having a crowd is a good thing. "They'll take everything they *might* want just so no one else can get it," she said.

After the initial run, stragglers picked over scraps like hyenas on a day-old zebra kill.

"Can you go any lower?" a customer asked about a knick-knack.

"Geez, Lady, it's only a nickel."

She hemmed and hawed and I didn't want to lose the sale so I gave her a nickel to take it.

One woman surveyed the leftovers, sniffed contemptuously, grabbed the box marked *FREE*, put it in the trunk of her Lincoln and putted off.

It went pretty well. The Redhead cleared $200, we sold all the heavy stuff, and I only had to haul one load back home.

Of course the victory is only temporary. We'll probably hit garage sales next week and buy it all back.

© Tony Bender, 1997

The Big Itch

All guys scratch. However, only Italians and baseball players are allowed to scratch in public.

A lot of folks don't know this but the thing that got Ducky Medwick into Cooperstown was he was MVP of the National League in 1937 while batting and catching one-handed. The other hand was rooting around in his jockstrap the entire season.

On a sad note, no matter how well Ducky played, no one ever shook his hand after the game because, well, they *knew* where it had been.

Since I am neither Italian or a major league baseball player, I am forced (by law) to wait until I am secure in the privacy of my home before I can scratch.

The Big Itch started a couple months ago. I'd take off my shirt and start scratching my left arm pit. Since I have been married more than five years, I was comfortable making ape sounds as I pawed my pit.

Suspicious it might be caused by a bad reaction to a new antiperspirant, I stopped using it altogether, thus experiencing the dreaded Medwick Treatment in the office. Customers would walk in, take a whiff of my pungent armpit and say, "Why don't I go back to my office and call you..."

Then my armpit turned an ugly purple. And it started to

really sting, forcing me to walk around with my arm raised all day.

Thus the rumor about my involvement in the white supremacy movement. I even had a couple John Birchers invite me to a tax protest meeting. (To any federal agents who may have overheard these conversations, let me reiterate, I personally feel I am not paying nearly enough in taxes.)

"Hey Ape Boy," The Redhead ordered after observing my nightly scratch, "Get to the doctor and get that checked!"

Having scoured the phone book unsuccessfully for an armpitologist, I called the local clinic and explained my problem.

My doctor suspected it might be a fungus but decided to scrape a sample from my armpit to send to the lab.

Let me say now that if I am ever shot down over hostile territory and subjected to vigorous armpit scraping, I will instantly renounce my U. S. citizenship and cheerfully accept a job in the rice paddies.

The idea I might have a fungus didn't get me too worried. In high school, I experienced every fungus known to man. They were all distributed in the locker room "powder box" in which everyone put their feet before putting on their socks.

I am sure that if that powder box—which is probably still in use today—was ever analyzed, it would be found to contain the customary fungi as well as botulism, e-coli, anthrax, bubonic plague and impetigo. I'm half-convinced that's where I picked up chicken pox.

The lab results were inconclusive, but still my physician was reasonably certain we were dealing with a fungus.

He wrote out the prescription but noted I could probably

buy the stuff right off the shelf.

"Just look for something to cure jock-itch."

Jock itch?

"That's right," he said looking at me curiously.

I squirmed.

Look Doc, I am 98 percent certain that I have never had a jock anywhere near my arm pit.

"Riiiiight," he said condescendingly as all doctors do when they are confronted with pathological liars and the insane.

No seriously.... I mean... Look, it could be something else, right?

"Riiiiight..." he agreed.

With just a fraction of my dignity still remaining, I rose to leave.

I was at the door when he spoke. "You realize, Tony, this matter is entirely confidential...."

Riiiiight....

© Tony Bender, 2000

Danger in a D Cup

Thank goodness for the Breast Police. They're gonna ban topless dancing in North Dakota's Hettinger County and I for one, am relieved. Breasts can be a dangerous thing. For example, in a recent edition of *Globe Magazine*, the headline read: ANNA NICOLE SMITH'S BOOB EXPLODES! I'm not kidding. By the way, Anna Nicole is the Guess Jeans® model who married a 235-year-old oil tycoon because she was deeply in love and has a thing for liver spots.

But back to the tragedy at hand. Maybe Dow Chemical accidentally filled Anna Nicole's implants with nitroglycerin. Or perhaps they were mined in an effort to ward off gropers. Possibly a top-secret military weapons experiment has reckless-ly gone awry. Regardless, the terms *blond bombshell* and *booby-trapped* are beginning to make sense to me now as is the suspicious demise of Anna Nicole's husband despite all indica-tions of impeccable health.

At any rate, my wife was so concerned, she bought the magazine at the local grocery store. I imagine women across the country were similarly concerned. I know I was. Later that day, when The Redhead hugged me, I panicked. "Hey, not so tight. One of those things might go off!"

Clearly, the Hettinger County Commission reacted correctly in moving to ban topless dancing at Dakota's Bar and Diner.

A breast explosion on a Saturday night could maim or seriously decapitate local men sitting in the front row. Not only is death a grave condition, but who needs that kind of publicity—CONGREGATION DECIMATED BY EXPLODING STRIPPER!

No, until scientists can assure us that breasts are 100 percent safe, I think it's in our best interest to stay as far away from them as possible. But if we're willing to risk it, I don't think there should be a cover charge.

But what of our wives and loved ones who are forced to walk around with time-bombs attached to their ribs?

The International Society of Hooter Inspection (ISHI) is concerned. "We are concerned," said a spokesman.

"But what can be done?" I asked.

"Encourage them not to jog," he advised. "Education is the first step to combating this problem."

That's why I wrote this column. To get the word out. And I also called my close friends to warn them. My first call was to Bev. "Bev, I don't want to alarm you, but your mother may be in extreme danger..."

Her Mom wears a size 55 Double G bra. Really. Now that's a Wonderbra. Bev's Dad says Double G stands for "Good God!" Sure, it seemed funny at the time, but now, if this woman starts doing jumping jacks, everything east of the Missouri could be wiped out.

Obviously, swift, decisive legislation is our only salvation against exploding glands. In Mandan, the law requires the Breast Police to be able to photograph all topless dancers. It makes a positive I.D. much easier if there is an explosion. Plus, let's face it, a lot of these cops are single.

I am also concerned about all those little babies out there whose life is at risk every time they breast feed. I contacted local breastfeeding officials about my concerns. "Have no fear, a spokesman said, "there has never been a documented case of a breast exploding during breastfeeding."

Yeah right.

Until the danger has passed, I'm sending The Redhead to live with her mother.

I think I'm doing the right thing.

© Tony Bender, 1996

Things Work Out

B ack in 1976, we all thought Whitey and Mary would get married. It was one of those certainties.

But Whitey has always been a tough read. I guess he felt a little smothered. Mary would have done anything for him, and the break-up nearly broke her heart.

I told The Redhead the story as we drove to Aberdeen last weekend. We'd left Baby Dylan with his maternal grandparents, to whom he'd just been introduced. Three weeks old, he'd be baptized in the morning. But tonight was our night. No way I could miss this.

"Gare Bear will be there," I told her. "And Al Cat, Woof Dog, Jaye-Bird, Katie, Muck and Balowsky..."

"Doesn't anyone have real names?" The Redhead asked.

"Gee, they all seemed like pretty normal names in high school."

My nickname was Bones, I told her. But upperclassmen would turn it into Boner once in a while. It's one of those things you try to ignore in high school. Let them know it bugs you and you'll carry the handle to the grave.

The worst offender was Mark VanDover. He had a way of saying 'Boner' that really got on my nerves. One night, a few years after graduation, I saw him at The Shed in Westport.

"BONER!" he called.

175

"PEE WEE!" I spat. That was his burden of a nickname.

I think we came to an agreement on nicknames that night.

We ran into him on the second floor of the church. He walked over in his tuxedo to shake my hand.

"TONY!"

"MARK! Nice to see you."

The Redhead smiled knowingly as I introduced her.

We'd seen Muck and Whitey in the parking lot. I could see them struggle to recognize me when we pulled up. It's been a lot of years. They were drinking beer. Some things never change.

I hadn't seen most of them since our 10-year reunion. Somehow, I expected them all to be the same old rude, supercilious, irresponsible friends I remembered.

Instead, I found myself looking at family photos, crushed in wallets. Some of their kids were there. It seemed everyone was successful, in a position of responsibility—even the goofballs you wouldn't have bet a plugged nickel on. That gang of friends that I'd always felt was exceptional, turned out to be exceptional after all. "My face hurts from grinning," I told The Redhead.

Katie snuck up from behind and gave me a big hug. She still has the prettiest big brown cow eyes. Her mom, Dottie, was there too. I can't count the times we raided her refrigerator in the dark of the night.

Jaye Bird was in charge of the guest book. Pretending to just put up with us, she sliced us with cutting remarks and then smiled that cover girl smile. She always seemed to be older than the rest of us, more mature. Her advice was always uncannily on target.

We sat by Muck and his wife, Bev, joking until the procession started. Mary was radiant in white, Whitey calm in his tuxedo. I held my breath when they got to the vows. After 20 years, you learn not to take anything for granted.

"Were you shocked when you got the invitation?" Mary asked in the receiving line.

"It was about time," I said.

At the reception, Woof Dog stripped off his trousers and pranced about in gym shorts. The Redhead and I visited with my old friends, and Gare Bear dragged her out to dance.

"Nobody looks like I thought they would," The Redhead said. "No one has any hair—except you."

Mary joked about having the oldest wedding party in the history of matrimony.

Whitey toured the room and eventually got to our table. We kibitzed and needled each other a bit. We'd been close friends. 'Thanks for coming, old man," he said.

"He's very charming," The Redhead remarked on the way back to her folks' home. Funny, I'd never thought of Whitey as charming. But I had to agree. He hadn't changed, except maybe for coming to his senses about Mary.

Things have a way of working out.

© Tony Bender, 1996

The Homecoming

He left in 1936. Back then, it seemed, everyone was going to Lodi. Even today, the population of Ashley transplants in Lodi might rival the former's population. You can, we have learned, take the North Dakotan out of North Dakota. But it is neigh impossible to take the North Dakota out of the North Dakotan. And who would want to? Best to leave alone that sturdy blend of you-betchas and dawn-to-dusk work ethic. That stoic common sense, the sense of loyalty.

He was 16 then. His family lived in that huge two and a half story house kitty-corner, northeast of the courthouse—the one The Redhead says we must have if it ever comes up for sale. His dad owned the store that in more recent times housed Family Clothing. It's big, made of fieldstone, and it was a general store back then. Groceries on one side. Dry goods on the other. But today, dust has settled, confident it will not be disturbed, thick on the floor. The paint is peeling in large sheets out back. Rightfully, so. Brick red paint on those perfectly bland field stones? Can you imagine?

Sixty-three years later, urged here by an all-school reunion, Walter walked through my door on Main Street. He was dapper and trim. I was sleepy, hollow-eyed, beard unkempt, wearing shorts, baggy faded T-shirt and sandals with no socks. It was an uncomfortable contrast.

178

Between the handshake and our first conversation, I was interrupted by a dozen phone calls and customers. As another gentleman waited, he and Walter struck up a conversation with that typical North Dakota directness.

Who are you?

"You're Wally Lippert!?"

They shared memories 30 years older than me. Walter had come alone. He'd lost his wife of 50 years in November, I overheard.

"It's tough," they agreed, searching each other's eyes before politely glancing away from the sorrow. We are the masters of understatement here on these prairies. We can summarize a lifetime's sorrow in two words. It's tough indeed.

The rush slowed, and Walter stayed and we talked about where the town had been, where it was and where it was going.

As we visited, I tried to imagine Walter's journey from North Dakota Depression times, to California businessman to grandfather of nine. And now, there was the pilgrimage here, alone. A plane trip. Alone. A rented car drive. Alone.

He'd stopped in, I think, because familiar faces were rare, and because mine, along with my column, had become a fixture in his more recent history.

I get a lot of that. They stop in, wait for me to say something clever, and when it doesn't happen, politely retreat, the fraud exposed.

I was glad we had a moment to speak. Good conversation is hard to come by.

Across the counter in the kitchen, as she chopped onions, I told The Redhead about this white-haired man with the kind eyes. "I think he needed a friend," I said, pleased that I had been chosen.

The next day, Walter brought his camera and had his picture taken with his "new buddy." We used the house camera to take a shot for me too.

During the parade, as I piloted the 1968 GTO we'd borrowed from The Redhead's dad, I spotted Walter, just a block or so from his old house. I tossed him a handful of candy. I hoped to spot him later to invite him out for burgers on the grill, but I didn't see him until Monday when he invited me to lunch at the cafe.

"Tell me about yourself," he asked as we waited for our meal. He listened to a summary of highs and lows and flawed life philosophies delivered with the conceit and uncertainty that plagues all writers, produces prose of variable quality and occasional horrid behaviors.

The great irony was, I told him, I got into the newspaper business because I loved to write. Now, I told him, there's not enough time to write. At 41, I feel a real sense of urgency. "I still have to write my novel," I told him.

"Oh, you have a long ways to go," he assured me. This from a man who has learned that life steers you; you do not steer it.

His perspective was a gift of solace.

Outside, I extended my hand. It would be the last time I would speak to him. He took my hand and then gave me a more appropriate hug.

I wished him many more years with his grandchildren. "Would you like to see a photo?" he asked. I would.

Surrounded by sons and their families, Walter was seated beside his wife, a handsome woman. The aneurism had taken her quickly, he said. "That's good," I said in my North Dakota wisdom.

Somehow, he looked smaller in the photo than I thought of him. Perhaps it is because she had been there to share the load. Flying solo, well, it's tough, we agreed.

He gave me the photo.

"I don't know when I'll have an excuse to come back here again," he said.

"Walter, I can be your excuse. You come back and stay with me," I told him.

As I walked back to my office, I realized that I had a family picture of my own at the office. If I hustled, and if he should tarry, I would get back to him with it.

I was late. I saw the nose of the gold rented car peek out two blocks west as I clutched the picture.

Two days later, as he headed to Bismarck for the plane ride home, he stopped in at my office.

I was late. A Dylan shoe-search had set me back ten minutes. I saw Walter walking down the street as I streaked past toward daycare. If I hustled back, I could catch him.

Two minutes later he was gone, his mission complete.

"He should have been here," Walter had joked at the office with my staff.

Perhaps. But poetic Casablanca endings are never inappropriate. Besides, I have·learned, you cannot steer life. Life—and three-year-olds—steer us.

"I'm going to miss him," I said wistfully, when I slumped into my chair at my computer.

Interesting. I had divined that he had needed a friend. What I did not realize—and what Walter knew—was that I had needed one too.

© Tony Bender, 2000

181

About the Author

Since 1990, when Tony Bender began publishing his award-winning weekly syndicated column, *"That's Life,"* he has become one of the most well-read writers in North Dakota.

Born in 1958 in Ashley, ND, Bender grew up in Frederick, SD, a tiny community on the ND-SD border, 26 miles north of Aberdeen, SD. After one year of journalism at SDSU in Brookings, SD, Bender, in 1977, embarked on a 15-year radio career including stops at KSDN and KKAA in Aberdeen and KQDJ in Jamestown, ND. In 1983, Bender moved to Denver where he worked at legendary radio stations KHOW and KIMN. His sense of adventure took him to Juneau, AK in 1986, where he starred at KTKU with his unique morning show featuring alter-egos like obnoxious newsman Irving R. Osgood and the unscrupulous Rev. Billy Joe Jim-Bob. In 1988, Bender was awarded the *"Goldie,"* a top honor from the Alaska Radio and Television Association, for his accomplishments at KTKU.

In 1989, Bender accepted a morning drive position at WBPR in Myrtle Beach, SC. Shortly after his arrival, Hurricane Hugo struck. While all other broadcast stations evacuated, Bender and his newsman elected to stay to broadcast to the many listeners who had not been able to evacuate in time. As the only station on the air for hundreds of miles delivering crucial information, the effort was widely applauded by SC officials and citizens.

In 1990, Bender returned to North Dakota to be closer to his family, accepting a position as news director at KYYY, Bismarck. In 1991, Bender turned to his first love, writing, when he took a position as a reporter at the *Williston (ND) Daily Herald*. Six months later he was offered the publishership of the floundering *Adams County Record* in Hettinger, ND. Bender, branded a maverick by some, sparked a resurgence in the newspaper, leading it to two *General Excellence Awards*, the highest honor from the North Dakota Newspaper Association. He served as executive news director for the parent company, Dickson Media, until 1997.

Bender's column has won seven newspaper association first place awards since 1990. He was presented the first-ever *NDNA First Amendment Award* in 2000, and he has garnered top honors for reporting, sports journalism, photography and design. He is a past winner of the *ND Heritage Writing Contest*. His writing has been published in *ND Outdoors*, *Publishers Auxiliary* and newspapers in many states.

Bender, and his wife, Julie, have two children, Dylan and India. The couple owns Redhead Publishing, which includes *The Wishek Star* and *Ashley Tribune*. They live in a rural home near Venturia, ND.